Classic Christmas Stories

By O. Henry
and other short story writers:
Georges Duhamel, Nathaniel Hawthorne, Willa
Cather, James Joyce, Guy de Maupassant, Anton
Chekhov, Bret Harte, William Dean Howells,
James Thurber

First Edition (2009)

Ancient Wisdom Publications

Sacramento, California, USA

Authors: O. Henry, Georges Duhamel, Nathaniel Hawthorne, Willa Cather, James Joyce, Guy de Maupassant, Anton Chekhov, Bret Harte, William Dean Howells, James Grover Thurber

ISBN 13   978-0-9824994-2-9

Printed in the United States of America

Table of Contents

I Réchoussat's Christmas

From Civilization: 1914-1917, by Georges Duhamel, 1918

RÉCHOUSSAT was repeating, with a weak and con-
strained laugh: "All the same, I tell you they won't come."

Corporal Têtard turned a deaf ear. He was arranging
his paraphernalia on a table: the compresses, the oil, the
rubber gloves which resembled slightly those of a fencer,
the probes, fastened to a tube like great pods of vanilla, a
basin of enameled iron that looked like an immense bean,
and a receptacle of glass with a big belly and a large
mouth, that looked like nothing at all.

Réchoussat assumed an air of unconcern: "They can
come or not as they choose. I don't care a hang."

Corporal Têtard shrugged his shoulders and answered:
"But I tell you they will come!"

The wounded man shook his head obstinately: "Here!
my poor fellow, no one comes here. All those people who
come down-stairs, well, they never come up here. That's
how it is, I tell you; but I don't care a hang."

"You may be certain they will come."

"And besides, I don't know why they've put me in this
little room, all alone."

"Probably because you have to be quiet."

"Whether they come or whether they don't come, it's all
the same to me." Réchoussat knitted his brows to show his
pride. Then he added, with a sigh: "You can go ahead with
that stunt of yours."

As a matter of fact, Corporal Têtard was just ready. He
had lighted a candle-end, and with a quick movement he
pulled down the sheets of the bed.

Réchoussat's body appeared, extraordinarily thin. But Têtard paid little attention to that, and Réchoussat himself had lived for three months on fairly good terms with his illness. He knew quite well that a fragment of shell in the back is always a serious matter, and that when yourarms and legs are paralyzed you can't go on putting things off from one day to another. Nevertheless, when the probe penetrated him, he uttered that consecrated phrase which he always repeated twice a day:

"What a wretched thing it is not to be able to do this business by yourself!"

The syringe was already in place. The glass receptacle was taking on the color of muddy amber, and a strong, penetrating odor was spreading through the chamber where the dying man lived the life of a recluse.

"That relieves you?" asked Têtard.

"Yes, it's a relief. It's six o'clock now and they haven't come yet. Lucky thing it's nothing to me!"

The corporal did not answer. With a bored air he was rubbing his rubber gloves one against the other. The flame of the candle, chained to its wick, leaped and strained like a poor prisoner that wanted to detach itself and rise, all by itself, in the darkness of the chamber, above that darkness, higher, still higher in the wintry sky, up into those regions where the sounds of this war of men were no longer to be heard. The wounded man and the attendant watched the flame without speaking, their eyes wide and empty. The glass receptacle slowly uttered a little liquid murmur. From second to second, the far-off guns sent a shudder through the windows, and each time the candle flame seemed to give a nervous leap.

"Takes long. You're not cold?" asked Têtard.

"As for the lower part of my body, I don't know what

cold is."

"That will come back."

"Surely it will come back. It's dead, but it's got to come alive again! I'm twenty-five years old: that's an age when you have some vigor in your flesh!"

The corporal nodded his head, embarrassed. Réchoussat seemed to him pretty far gone: he had great sores wherever his body touched the bed, and they had put him by himself to conceal the spectacle of his slow agony from the sight of his more fortunate comrades.

A long moment passed. The silence was too heavy for the nothings they had to say. Then, as if continuing some discussion within himself, Réchoussat suddenly went on:

"Just the same, you know, it doesn't take much to please me. If they had only come for two minutes!"

"Keep still!" said Têtard. "Keep still!"

He strained his ear toward the door. There was a confused noise coming down the corridor, with sudden shadows and gusts of fresh air.

"Hello! there they are!" said the attendant.

Réchoussat stretched his neck.

"Bah! I tell you it isn't so!"

All at once a supernatural light, with rich red and golden reflections, an unheard of, a fairylike light had burst out in the corridor. The opposite wall appeared. Usually it was as gray as the thoughts of December; suddenly it had the splendor of an Oriental palace or the gown of a princess. All this light was mingled with sound, a sound of voices and laughter. One could not distinguish any one person singing, but all together the sound seemed like some great song. Réchoussat, who could not move himself, strained his neck and lifted his hands a little above the sheet, as if he wished to touch that beautiful

6

sound and that beautiful light.

"You see, you see!" said Têtard. "I told you they'd come."

Of a sudden everything seemed to be on fire. Something had just stopped before the door--a tree, a real fir-tree from the woods, set up in a green box. There were so many little lamps and so many pink candles on its branches that it looked like an enormous torch. The little room, like a heart that is too happy, seemed as if it would burst with all this light inside of it. And there was something more wonderful still: the Three Wise Men entered. They were Sorri, the Senegalese sharp-shooter, Moussa, and Cazin. They wore mantles of Andrinople and long white beards made with cotton and bandages.

They all entered and moved to the other end of Réchoussat's room. Sorri carried a package with a favor in it; Moussa brandished two cigars and Cazin a bottle of champagne. All three of them saluted ceremoniously, as they had been taught to do, and Réchoussat suddenly found himself with a box of bonbons in his right hand, two cigars in his left, and a sparkling bottle on his little table. He said:

"Ah, no, boys! That's too much! No, no, boys!"

Moussa and Cazin laughed, Sorri showed his teeth, and all the bad odor of the room was gone, as if only a little light had been needed to drive it away.

"Ah, no, boys!" repeated Réchoussat. "I don't smoke, but I'll keep the cigars as a souvenir. Pass me the wine!"

Sorri took the bottle in both hands and presented it as if it were a sacred cup. Réchoussat drank slowly, saying:

"That's the real stuff! What good wine!"

There were more than twenty faces at the door, and all the faces were laughing like the gentle, naive face of Réchoussat himself.

Then followed a regular sunset. The marvelous tree went off, jerkily, down the corridor. The Three Wise Men vanished, with their trailing mantles and their cotton beards. Réchoussat still held his bottle in his hand and looked at the candle as if all the lights had remained in this one. He laughed softly, as he repeated: "That surely is real wine!" Then he went on laughing a little, without saying anything.

Very softly the darkness slipped back into the room and spread itself everywhere, like a familiar animal disturbed from its customary place.

Something else, something dreary, stole back everywhere with it, the odor of Réchoussat's illness. A murmurous silence settled over everything in the room, like dust. The face of the wounded man ceased to reflect the splendor of the festive tree; he lowered his eyes, looked at the bed, at those thin, ulcerated legs which were his legs, at the glass jar full of muddy liquid, at the probe,-- at all these incomprehensible things, and he said, stammering with astonishment:

"But . . . but . . . What's the meaning of all this? What's the meaning of all this?"

II   The Christmas Banquet

FROM THE UNPUBLISHED "ALLEGORIES OF THE
HEART"By Nathaniel Hawthorne, 1804-1864

"I HAVE HERE attempted," said Roderick, unfolding a
few sheets of manuscript, as he sat with Rosina and the
sculptor in the summer-house--"I have attempted to seize
hold of a personage who glides past me, occasionally, in
my walk through life. My former sad experience, as you
know, has gifted me with some degree of insight into the
gloomy mysteries of the human heart, through which I
have wandered like one astray in a dark cavern, with his
torch fast flickering to extinction. But this man--this class
of men--is a hopeless puzzle."

"Well, but propound him," said the sculptor. "Let us
have an idea of him, to begin with."

"Why, indeed," replied Roderick, "he is such a being as I
could conceive you to carve out of marble, and some yet
unrealized perfection of human science to endow with an
exquisite mockery of intellect; but still there lacks the last
inestimable touch of a divine Creator. He looks like a man,
and, perchance, like a better specimen of man than you
ordinarily meet. You might esteem him wise--he is capable
of cultivation and refinement, and has at least an external
conscience--but the demands that spirit makes upon spirit,
are precisely those to which he cannot respond. When, at
last, you come close to him, you find him chill and unsub-
stantial--a mere vapor."

"I believe," said Rosina, "I have a glimmering idea of
what you mean."

"Then be thankful," answered her husband, smiling;
"but do not anticipate any further illumination from what I

am about to read. I have here imagined such a man to be--what, probably, he never is--conscious of the deficiency in his spiritual organization. Methinks the result would be a sense of cold unreality, wherewith he would go shivering through the world, longing to exchange his load of ice for any burthen of real grief that fate could fling upon a human being."

Contenting himself with this preface, Roderick began to read.

In a certain old gentleman's last will and testament, there appeared a bequest, which, as his final thought and deed, was singularly in keeping with a long life of melancholy eccentricity. He devised a considerable sum for establishing a fund, the interest of which was to be expended, annually forever, in preparing a Christmas Banquet for ten of the most miserable persons that could be found. It seemed not to be the testator's purpose to make these half-a-score of sad hearts merry, but to provide that the stern or fierce expression of human discontent should not be drowned, even for that one holy and joyful day, amid the acclamations of festal gratitude which all Christendom sends up. And he desired, likewise, to perpetuate his own remonstrance against the earthly course of Providence, and his sad and sour dissent from those systems of religion or philosophy which either find sunshine in the world, or draw it down from heaven.

The task of inviting the guests, or of selecting among such as might advance their claims to partake of this dismal hospitality, was confided to the two trustees or stewards of the fund. These gentlemen, like their deceased friend, were sombre humorists, who made it their principal occupation to number the sable threads in the web of human life, and drop all the golden ones out of the reckoning. They performed their present office with integrity and judgment. The aspect of the assembled company, on the day of the first festival, might not, it is true, have satisfied every beholder that these were especially the individuals, chosen forth from all the world, whose griefs were worthy to stand as indicators of the mass of human suffering. Yet, after due consideration, it could not be disputed that here was a variety of hopeless discomfort, which, if it sometimes arose from causes apparently inadequate, was thereby only the shrewder imputation against the nature and mechanism of life.

The arrangements and decorations of the banquet were probably intended to signify that death-in-life which had been the testator's definition of existence. The hall, illuminated by torches, was hung round with curtains of deep and dusky purple, and adorned with branches of cypress and wreaths of artificial flowers, imitative of such as used to be strewn over the dead. A sprig of parsley was laid by every plate. The main reservoir of wine was a sepulchral urn of silver, whence the liquor was distributed around the table in small vases, accurately copied from those that held the tears of ancient mourners. Neither had the stewards--if it were their taste that arranged these details-- forgotten the fantasy of the old Egyptians, who seated a skeleton at every festive board, and mocked their own merriment with the imperturbable grin of a death's-head.

Such a fearful guest, shrouded in a black mantle, sat now at the head of the table. It was whispered, I know not with what truth, that the testator himself had once walked the visible world with the machinery of that same skeleton, and that it was one of the stipulations of his will, that he should thus be permitted to sit, from year to year, at the

11

banquet which he had instituted. If so, it was perhaps covertly implied that he had cherished no hopes of bliss beyond the grave to compensate for the evils which he felt or imagined here. And if, in their bewildered conjectures as to the purpose of earthly existence, the banqueters should throw aside the veil, and cast an inquiring glance at this figure of death, as seeking thence the solution otherwise unattainable, the only reply would be a stare of the vacant eye-caverns, and a grin of the skeleton-jaws. Such was the response that the dead man had fancied himself to receive, when he asked of Death to solve the riddle of his life; and it was his desire to repeat it when the guests of his dismal hospitality should find themselves perplexed with the same question.

"What means that wreath?" asked several of the company, while viewing the decorations of the table.

They alluded to a wreath of cypress, which was held on high by a skeleton-arm, protruding from within the black mantle.

"It is a crown," said one of the stewards, "not for the worthiest, but for the wofullest, when he shall prove his claim to it."

The guest earliest bidden to the festival, vvas a man of soft and gentle character, who had not energy to struggle against the heavy despondency to which his temperament rendered him liable; and therefore, with nothing outwardly to excuse him from happiness, he had spent a life of quiet misery, that made his blood torpid, and weighed upon his breath, and sat like a ponderous night-fiend upon every throb of his unresisting heart.

His wretchedness seemed as deep as his original nature, if not identical with it. It was the misfortune of a second guest to cherish within his bosom a diseased heart, which

had become so wretchedly sore, that the continual and unavoidable rubs of the world, the blow of an enemy, the
careless jostle of a stranger, and even the faithful and loving touch of a friend, alike made ulcers in it. As is the habit
of people thus afflicted, he found his chief employment in
exhibiting these miserable sores to any who would give
themselves the pain of viewing them.

A third guest was a hypochondriac, whose imagination
wrought necromancy in his outward and inward world,
and caused him to see monstrous faces in the household
fire, and dragons in the clouds of sunset, and fiends in the
guise of beautiful women, and something ugly or wicked
beneath all the pleasant surfaces of nature. His neighbor at
table was one who, in his early youth, had trusted mankind too much, and hoped too highly in their behalf, and,
in meeting with many disappointments, had become desperately soured.

For several years back, this misanthrope had employed
himself in accumulating motives for hating and despising
his race--such as murder, lust, treachery, ingratitude, faith-
lessness of trusted friends, instinctive vices of children,
impurity of women, hidden guilt in men of saint-like as-
pect--and, in short, all manner of black realities that sought
to decorate themselves with outward grace or glory. But,
at every atrocious fact that was added to his catalogue--at
every increase of the sad knowledge which he spent his
life to collect--the native impulses of the poor man's loving
and confiding heart made him groan with anguish. Next,
with his heavy brow bent downward, there stole into the
hall a man naturally earnest and impassioned, who, from
his immemorial infancy, had felt the consciousness of a
high message to the world, but, essaying to deliver it, had
found either no voice or form of speech, or else no ears to

listen.

Therefore his whole life was a bitter questioning of himself--"Why have not men acknowledged my mission? Am I not a self-deluding fool? What business have I on earth? Where is my grave?" Throughout the festival, he quaffed frequent draughts from the sepulchral urn of wine, hoping thus to quench the celestial fire that tortured his own breast, and could not benefit his race.

Then there entered--having flung away a ticket for a ball--a gay gallant of yesterday, who had found four or five wrinkles in his brow, and more grey hairs than he could well number, on his head. Endowed with sense and feeling, he had nevertheless spent his youth in folly, but had reached at last that dreary point in life, where Folly quits us of her own accord, leaving us to make friends with Wisdom if we can. Thus, cold and desolate, he had come to seek Wisdom at the banquet, and wondered if the skeleton were she. To eke out the company, the stewards had invited a distressed poet from his home in the alms-house, and a melancholy idiot from the street corner.

The latter had just the glimmering of sense that was sufficient to make him conscious of a vacancy, which the poor fellow, all his life long, had mistily sought to fill up with intelligence, wandering up and down the streets, and groaning miserably, because his attempts were ineffec-tual.. The only lady in the hall was one who had fallen short of absolute and perfect beauty, merely by the trifling defect of a slight cast in her left eye. But this blemish, min-ute as it was, so shocked the pure ideal of her soul, rather than her vanity, that she passed her life in solitude, and veiled her countenance even from her own gaze. So the skeleton sat shrouded at one end of the table, and this poor lady at the other.

One other guest remains to be described. He was a young man of smooth brow, fair cheek, and fashionable mien. So far as his exterior developed him, he might much more suitably have found a place at some merry Christmas table, than have been numbered among the blighted, fate-stricken, fancy-tortured set of ill-starred banqueters. Murmurs arose among the guests, as they noted the glance of general scrutiny which the intruder threw over his companions. What had he to do among them; Why did not the skeleton of the dead founder of the feast unbend its rattling joints, arise, and motion the unwelcome stranger from the board? "Shameful!" said the morbid man, while a new ulcer broke out in his heart. "He comes to mock us!--we shall be the jest of his tavern friends!--he will make a farce of our miseries, and bring it out upon the stage!"

"Oh, never mind him!" said the hypochondriac, smiling sourly. "He shall feast from yonder tureen of viper soup, and if there is a fricassee of scorpions on the table, pray let him have his share of it. For the dessert, he shall taste the apples of Sodom. Then, if he like our Christmas fare, let him return again next year!"

"Trouble him not," murmured the melancholy man, with gentleness. "What matters it whether the consciousness of misery come a few years sooner or later; If this youth deem himself happy now, yet let him sit with us, for the sake of the wretchedness to come."

The poor idiot approached the young man, with that mournful aspect of vacant inquiry which his face continually wore, and which caused people to say that he was always in search of his missing wits. After no little examination, he touched the stranger's hand, but immediately drew back his own, shaking his head and shivering.

"Cold, cold, cold!" muttered the idiot.

15

The young man shivered too--and smiled.

"Gentlemen--and you, madam,"--said one of the stewards of the festival, "do not conceive so ill, either of our caution or judgment, as to imagine that we have admitted this young stranger--Gervayse Hastings by name--without a full investigation and thoughtful balance of his claims. Trust me, not a guest at the table is better entitled to his seat."

The steward's guarantee was perforce satisfactory. The company, therefore, took their places, and addressed themselves to the serious business of the feast, but were soon disturbed by the hypochondriac, who thrust back his chair, complaining that a dish of stewed toads and vipers was set before him, and that there was green ditch-water in his cup of wine. This mistake being amended, he quietly resumed his seat. The wine, as it flowed freely from the sepulchral urn, seemed to come imbued with all gloomy inspirations; so that its influence was not to cheer, but either to sink the revellers into a deeper melancholy, or elevate their spirits to an enthusiasm of wretchedness.

The conversation was various. They told sad stories about people who might have been worthy guests at such a festival as the present. They talked of grisly incidents in human history; of strange crimes, which, if truly considered, were but convulsions of agony; of some lives that had been altogether wretched, and of others, which, wearing a general semblance of happiness, had yet been deformed, sooner or later, by misfortune, as by the intrusion of a grim face at a banquet; of death-bed scenes, and what dark intimations might be gathered from the words of dying men; of suicide, and whether the more eligible mode were by halter, knife, poison, drowning, gradual starvation, or the fumes of charcoal.

The majority of the guests, as is the custom with people thoroughly and profoundly sick at heart, were anxious to make their own woes the theme of discussion, and prove themselves most excellent in anguish. The misanthropist went deep into the philosophy of evil, and wandered about in the darkness, with now and then a gleam of discolored light hovering on ghastly shapes and horrid scenery. Many a miserable thought, such as men have stumbled upon from age to age, did he now rake up again, and gloat over it as an inestimable gem, a diamond, a treasure far preferable to those bright, spiritual revelations of a better world, which are like precious stones from heaven's pavement. And then, amid his lore of wretchedness, he hid his face and wept.

It was a festival at which the woful man of Uz might suitably have been a guest, together with all, in each succeeding age, who have tasted deepest of the bitterness of life. And be it said, too, that every son or daughter of woman, however favored with happy fortune, might, at one sad moment or another, have claimed the privilege of a stricken heart, to sit down at this table. But, throughout the feast, it was remarked that the young stranger, Gervayse Hastings, was unsuccessful in his attempts to catch its pervading spirit. At any deep, strong thought that found utterance, and which was torn out, as it were, from the saddest recesses of human consciousness, he looked mystified and bewildered; even more than the poor idiot, who seemed to grasp at such things with his earnest heart, and thus occasionally to comprehend them. The young man's conversation was of a colder and lighter kind, often brilliant, but lacking the powerful characteristics of a nature that had been developed by suffering.

"Sir," said the misanthropist, bluntly, in reply to some

observation by Gervayse Hastings, "pray do not address me again. We have no right to talk together. Our minds have nothing in common. By what claim you appear at this banquet, I cannot guess; but methinks, to a man who could say what you have just now said, my companions and myself must seem no more than shadows, flickering on the wall. And precisely such a shadow are you to us!"

The young man smiled and bowed, but drawing himself back in his chair, he buttoned his coat over his breast, as if the banqueting-hall were growing chill. Again the idiot fixed his melancholy stare upon the youth, and murmured--"Cold! cold! cold!"

The banquet drew to its conclusion, and the guests departed. Scarcely had they stepped across the threshold of the hall, when the scene that had there passed seemed like the vision of a sick fancy, or an exhalation from a stagnant heart. Now and then, however, during the year that ensued, these melancholy people caught glimpses of one another, transient, indeed, but enough to prove that they walked the earth with the ordinary allotment of reality. Sometimes, a pair of them came face to face, while stealing through the evening twilight, enveloped in their sable cloaks. Sometimes, they casually met in church-yards. Once, also, it happened, that two of the dismal banqueters mutually started, at recognizing each other in the noon-day sunshine of a crowded street, stalking there like ghosts astray. Doubtless, they wondered why the skeleton did not come abroad at noonday, too!

But, whenever the necessity of their affairs compelled these Christmas guests into the bustling world, they were sure to encounter the young man, who had so unaccountably been admitted to the festival. They saw him among the gay and fortunate; they caught the sunny sparkle of his eye; they heard the light and careless tones of his voice--and muttered to themselves, with such indignation as only the aristocracy of wretchedness could kindle:--"The traitor! The vile impostor! Providence, in its own good time, may give him a right to feast among us!" But the young man's unabashed eye dwelt upon their gloomy figures, as they passed him, seeming to say, perchance with somewhat of a sneer--"First, know my secret!--then, measure your claims with mine!"

The step of Time stole onward, and soon brought merry Christmas round again, with glad and solemn worship in the churches, and sports, games, festivals, and everywhere the bright face of Joy beside the household fire. Again, likewise, the hall, with its curtains of dusky purple, was illuminated by the death-torches, gleaming on the sepulchral decorations of the banquet. The veiled skeleton sat in state, lifting the cypress wreath above its head, as the guerdon of some guest, illustrious in the qualifications which there claimed precedence. As the stewards deemed the world inexhaustible in misery, and were desirous of recognizing it in all its forms, they had not seen fit to re-assemble the company of the former year. New faces now threw their gloom across the table.

There was a man of nice conscience, who bore a blood-stain in his heart--the death of a fellow-creature--which, for his more exquisite torture, had chanced with such a peculiarity of circumstances, that he could not absolutely determine whether his will had entered into the deed, or not. Therefore, his whole life was spent in the agony of an inward trial for murder, with a continual sifting of the details of his terrible calamity, until his mind had no longer any thought, nor his soul any emotion, disconnected with it.

There was a mother, too--a mother once, but a desolation now--who, many years before, had gone out on a pleasure-party, and, returning, found her infant smothered in its little bed. And ever since she had been tortured with the fantasy, that her buried baby lay smothering in its coffin. Then there was an aged lady, who had lived from time immemorial with a constant tremor quivering through her frame. It was terrible to discern her dark shadow tremulous upon the wall; her lips, likewise, were tremulous; and the expression of her eyes seemed to indicate that her soul was trembling too.

Owing to the bewilderment and confusion which made almost a chaos of her intellect, it was impossible to discover what dire misfortune had thus shaken her nature to its depths; so that the stewards had admitted her to the table, not from any acquaintance with her history, but on the safe testimony of her miserable aspect. Some surprise was expressed at the presence of a bluff, red-faced gentleman, a certain Mr. Smith, who had evidently the fat of many a rich feast within him, and the habitual twinkle of whose eye betrayed a disposition to break forth into uproarious laughter, for little cause or none.

It turned out, however, that, with the best possible flow of spirits, our poor friend was afflicted with a physical disease of the heart, which threatened instant death on the slightest cachinnatory indulgence, or even that titillation of the bodily frame, produced by merry thoughts. In this dilemma, he had sought admittance to the banquet, on the ostensible plea of his irksome and miserable state, but, in reality, with the hope of imbibing a life-preserving melancholy.

A married couple had been invited, from a motive of bitter humor; it being well understood, that they rendered each other unutterably miserable whenever they chanced to meet, and therefore must necessarily be fit associates at the festival. In contrast with these, was another couple, still unmarried, who had interchanged their hearts in early life, but had been divided by circumstances as impalpable as morning mist, and kept apart so long, that their spirits now found it impossible to meet. Therefore, yearning for communion, yet shrinking from one another, and choosing none beside, they felt themselves companionless in life, and looked upon eternity as a boundless desert.

Next to the skeleton sat a mere son of earth--a haunter of the Exchange--a gatherer of shining dust--a man whose life's record was in his leger, and whose soul's prison-house, the vaults of the bank where he kept his deposits. This person had been greatly perplexed at his invitation, deeming himself one of the most fortunate men in the city; but the stewards persisted in demanding his presence, assuring him that he had no conception how miserable he was.

And now appeared a figure, which we must acknowledge as our acquaintance of the former festival. It was Gervayse Hastings, whose presence had then caused so much question and criticism, and who now took his place with the composure of one vvhose claims were satisfactory to himself, and must needs be allowed by others. Yet his easy and unruffled face betrayed no sorrow. The well-skilled beholders gazed a moment into his eyes, and shook their heads, to miss the unuttered sympathy--the counter-sign, never to be falsified--of those whose hearts are cavern-mouths, through which they descend into a region of illimitable wo, and recognize other wanderers there.

"Who is this youth?" asked the man with a blood-stain on his conscience. "Surely he has never gone down into the depths! I know all the aspects of those who have passed through the dark valley. By what right is he among us?"

"Ah, it is a sinful thing to come hither without a sorrow," murmured the aged lady, in accents that partook of the eternal tremor which pervaded her whole being. "Depart, young man! Your soul has never been shaken; and therefore I tremble so much the more to look at you."

"His soul shaken! No; I'll answer for it," said bluff Mr. Smith, pressing his hand upon his heart, and making himself as melancholy as he could, for fear of a fatal explosion of laughter. "I know the lad well; he has as fair prospects as any young man about town, and has no more right among us, miserable creatures, than the child unborn. He never was miserable, and probably never will be!"

"Our honored guests," interposed the stewards, "pray have patience with us, and believe, at least, that our deep veneration for the sacredness of this solemnity would preclude any wilful violation of it. Receive this young man to your table. It may not be too much to say, that no guest here would exchange his own heart for the one that beats within that youthful bosom!"

"I'd call it a bargain, and gladly too," muttered Mr. Smith, with a perplexing mixture of sadness and mirthful conceit. "A plague upon their nonsense! My own heart is the only really miserable one in the company--it will certainly be the death of me at last!"

Nevertheless, as on the former occasion, the judgment of the stewards being without appeal, the company sat down. The obnoxious guest made no more attempt to obtrude his conversation on those about him, but appeared to listen to the table-talk with peculiar assiduity, as if some inestimable secret, otherwise beyond his reach, might be conveyed in a casual word. And, in tmth, to those who could understand and value it, there was rich matter in the upgushings and outpourings of these initiated souls, to whom sorrow had been a talisman, admitting them into spiritual depths which no other spell can open. Sometimes, out of the midst of densest gloom, there flashed a momentary radiance, pure as crystal, bright as the flame of stars, and shedding such a glow upon the mystery of life, that the guests were ready to exclaim, "Surely the riddle is on the point of being solved!" At such illuminated intervals, the saddest mourners felt it to be revealed, that mortal griefs are but shadowy and external; no more than the sable robes, voluminously shrouding a certain divine reality, and thus indicating what might otherwise be altogether invisible to mortal eye.

"Just now," remarked the trembling old woman, "I seemed to see beyond the outside. And then my everlasting tremor passed away!"

"Would that I could dwell always in these momentary gleams of light!" said the man of stricken conscience. "Then the blood-stain in my heart would be washed clean away."

This strain of conversation appeared so unintelligibly absurd to good Mr. Smith, that he burst into precisely the fit of laughter which his physicians had warned him against, as likely to prove instantaneously fatal. In effect, he fell back in his chair, a corpse with a broad grin upon his face; while his ghost, perchance, remained beside it, bewildered at its unpremeditated exit. This catastrophe, of course, broke up the festival.

"How is this? You do not tremble?" observed the tremulous old woman to Gervayse Hastings, who was gazing at the dead man with singular intentness. "Is it not awful to see him so suddenly vanish out of the midst of life--this man of flesh and blood, whose earthly nature was so warm and strong? There is a never-ending tremor in my soul; but it trembles afresh at this! And you are calm!"

"Would that he could teach me somewhat!" said Gervayse Hastings, drawing a long breath. "Men pass before me like shadows on the wall--their actions, passions, feelings, are flickering of the light--and then they vanish! Neither the corpse, nor yonder skeleton, nor this old woman's everlasting tremor, can give me what I seek."

And then the company departed.

We cannot linger to narrate, in such detail, more circumstances of these singular festivals, which, in accordance with the founder's will, continued to be kept with the regularity of an established institution. In process of time, the stewards adopted the custom of inviting, from far and near, those individuals whose misfortunes were prominent above other men's, and whose mental and moral development might, therefore, be supposed to possess a corresponding interest. The exiled noble of the French Revolution, and the broken soldier of the Empire, were alike represented at the table. Fallen monarchs, wandering about the earth, have found places at that forlorn and miserable feast.

The statesman, when his party flung him off, might, if he chose it, be once more a great man for the space of a single banquet. Aaron Burr's name appears on the record, at a period when his ruin--the profoundest and most striking, with more of moral circumstance in it than that of almost any other man--was complete, in his lonely age. Stephen Girard, when his wealth weighed upon him like a mountain, once sought admittance of his own accord. It is not probable, however, that these men had any lessons to teach in the lore of discontent and misery, which might not equally well have been studied in the common walks of life. Illustrious unfortunates attract a wider sympathy, not because their griefs are more intense, but because, being set on lofty pedestals, they the better serve mankind as instances and by-words of calamity.

It concerns our present purpose to say that, at each successive festival, Gervayse Hastings showed his face, gradually changing from the smooth beauty of his youth to the thoughtful comeliness of manhood, and thence to the bald, impressive dignity of age. He was the only individual invariably present. Yet, on every occasion, there were murmurs, both from those who knew his character and position, and from them whose hearts shrank back, as denying his companionship in their mystic fraternity.

"Who is this impassive man?" had been asked a hundred times. "Has he suffered? Has he sinned? There are no traces of either. Then wherefore is he here?"

"You must inquire of the stewards, or of himself," was the constant reply. "We seem to know him well, here in our city, and know nothing of him but what is creditable and fortunate. Yet hither he comes, year after year, to this gloomy banquet, and sits among the guests like a marble statue. Ask yonder skeleton--perhaps that may solve the riddle!"

It was, in truth, a wonder. The life of Gervayse Hastings was not merely a prosperous, but a brilliant one. Everything had gone well with him. He was wealthy, far beyond the expenditure that was required by habits of magnificence, a taste of rare purity and cultivation, a love of travel, a scholar's instinct to collect a splendid library, and, moreover, what seemed a munificent liberality to the distressed. He had sought domestic happiness, and not vainly, if a lovely and tender wife, and children of fair promise, could insure it. He had, besides, ascended above the limit which separates the obscure from the distinguished, and had won a stainless reputation in affairs of the widest public importance.

Not that he was a popular character, or had within him the mysterious attributes which are essential to that species of success. To the public, he was a cold abstraction, wholly destitute of those rich hues of personality, that living warmth, and the peculiar faculty of stamping his own heart's impression on a multitude of hearts, by which the people recognize their favorites. And it must be owned that, after his most intimate associates had done their best to know him thoroughly, and love him warmly, they were startled to find how little hold he had upon their affections. They approved--they admired--but still, in those moments when the human spirit most craves reality, they shrank back from Gervayse Hastings, as powerless to give them what they sought. It was the feeling of distrustful regret, with which we should draw back the hand, after extending it, in an illusive twilight, to grasp the hand of a shadow upon the wall.

As the superficial fervency of youth decayed, this peculiar effect of Gervayse Hastings' character grew more perceptible. His children, when he extended his arms, came coldly to his knees, but never climbed them of their own accord. His wife wept secretly, and almost adjudged herself a criminal, because she shivered in the chill of his bosom. He, too, occasionally appeared not unconscious of the chillness of his moral atmosphere, and willing, if it might be so, to warm himself at a kindly fire. But age stole onward, and benumbed him more and more.

As the hoar-frost began to gather on him, his wife went to her grave, and was doubtless warmer there; his children either died, or were scattered to different homes of their own; and old Gervayse Hastings, unscathed by grief--alone, but needing no companionship--continued his steady walk through life, and still, on every Christmas-day, attended at the dismal banquet. His privilege as a guest had become prescriptive now. Had he claimed the head of the table, even the skeleton would have been ejected from its seat.

Finally, at the merry Christmas-tide, when he had numbered four-score years complete, this pale, high-browed, marble-featured old man once more entered the long-frequented hall, with the same impassive aspect that had called forth so much dissatisfied remark at his first attendance. Time, except in matters merely external, had done nothing for him, either of good or evil. As he took his place, he threw a calm, inquiring glance around the table, as if to ascertain whether any guest had yet appeared, after so many unsuccessful banquets, who might impart to him the mystery--the deep, warm secret--the life within the life--which, whether manifested in joy or sorrow, is what gives substance to a world of shadows.

"My friends," said Gervayse Hastings, assuming a position which his long conversance with the festival caused to appear natural, "you are welcome! I drink to you all in this cup of sepulchral wine."

The guests replied courteously, but still in a manner that proved them unable to receive the old man as a member of their sad fraternity. It may be well to give the reader an idea of the present company at the banquet.

One was formerly a clergyman, enthusiastic in his profession, and apparently of the genuine dynasty of those old Puritan divines whose faith in their calling, and stern exercise of it, had placed them among the mighty of the earth. But, yielding to the speculative tendency of the age, he had gone astray from the firm foundation of an ancient faith, and wandered into a cloud region, where everything was misty and deceptive, ever mocking him with a semblance of reality, but still dissolving when he flung himself upon it for support and rest. His instinct and early training demanded something steadfast; but, looking forward, he beheld vapors piled on vapors, and, behind him, an impassable gulf between the man of yesterday and to-day; on the borders of which he paced to and fro, sometimes wringing his hands in agony, and often making his own wo a theme of scornful merriment. This, surely, was a miserable man.

Next, there was a theorist--one of a numerous tribe, although he deemed himself unique since the creation--a theorist, who had conceived a plan by which all the wretchedness of earth, moral and physical, might be done away, and the bliss of the millennium at once accomplished. But, the incredulity of mankind debarring him from action, he was smitten with as much grief as if the whole mass of wo which he was denied the opportunity to remedy, were crowded into his own bosom. A plain old man in black attracted much of the company's notice, on the supposition tht he was no other than Father Miller, who, it seemed, had given himself up to despair at the tedious delay of the final conflagration.

Then there was a man distinguished for native pride and obstinacy, who, a little while before, had possessed immense wealth, and held the control of a vast moneyed interest, which he had wielded in the same spirit as a despotic monarch would wield the power of his empire, carrying on a tremendous moral warfare, the roar and tremor of which was felt at every fireside in the land. At length came a crushing ruin--a total overthrow of fortune, power, and character--the effect of which on his imperious, and, in many respects, noble and lofty nature, might have entitled him to a place, not merely at our festival, but among the peers of Pandemonium.

There was a modern philanthropist, who had become so deeply sensible of the calamities of thousands and millions of his fellow creatures, and of the impracticableness of any general measures for their relief, that he had no heart to do what little good lay immediately within his power, but contented himself with being miserable for sympathy. Near him sat a gentleman in a predicament hitherto unprecedented, but of which the present epoch, probably, affords numerous examples. Ever since he was of capacity to read a newspaper, this person had prided himself on his consistent adherence to one political party, but, in the confusion of these latter days, had got bewildered, and knew not whereabouts his party was.

This wretched condition, so morally desolate and disheartening to a man who has long accustomed himself to merge his individuality in the mass of a great body, can only be conceived by such as have experienced it. His next companion was a popular orator who had lost his voice, and--as it was pretty much all that he had to lose--had fallen into a state of hopeless melancholy. The table was likewise graced by two of the gentler sex--one, a half-starved, consumptive seamstress, the representative of thousands just as wretched; the other, a woman of unemployed energy, who found herself in the world with nothing to achieve, nothing to enjoy, and nothing even to suffer. She had, therefore, driven herself to the verge of madness by dark broodings over the wrongs of her sex, and its exclusion from a proper field of action.

The roll of guests being thus complete, a side-table had been set for three or four disappointed office-seekers with hearts as sick as death, whom the stewards had admitted, partly because their calamities really entitled them to entrance here, and partly that they were in especial need of a good dinner. There was likewise a homeless dog, with his tail between his legs, licking up the crumbs and gnawing the fragments of the feast--such a melancholy cur as one sometimes sees about the streets, without a master, and willing to follow the first that will accept his service.

In their own way, these were as wretched a set of people as ever had assembled at the festival. There they sat, with the veiled skeleton of the founder, holding aloft the cypress wreath, at one end of the table; and at the other, wrapt in furs, the withered figure of Gervayse Hastings, stately, calm, and cold, impressing the company with awe, yet so little interesting their sympathy, that he might have vanished into thin air, without their once exclaiming-- "Whither is he gone?"

"Sir," said the philanthropist, addressing the old man, "you have been so long a guest at this annual festival, and have thus been conversant with so many varieties of human affliction, that, not improbably, you have thence derived some great and important lessons. How blessed were your lot, could you reveal a secret by which all this mass of wo might be removed!"

"I know of but one misfortune," answered Gervayse Hastings, quietly, "and that is my own."

"Your own!" rejoined the philanthropist. "And, looking back on your serene and prosperous life, how can you claim to be the sole unfortunate of the human race?"

"You will not understand it," replied Gervayse Hastings, feebly, and with a singular inefficiency of pronunciation, and sometimes putting one word for an-other. "None have understood it--not even those who experience the like. It is a chillness--a want of earnestness--a feeling as if what should be my heart were a thing of va-por--a haunting perception of unreality! Thus, seeming to possess all that other men have--all that men aim at--I have really possessed nothing, neither joys nor griefs. All things--all persons--as was truly said to me at this table long and long ago--have been like shadows flickering on the wall. It was so with my wife and children-- with those who seemed my friends: it is so with yourselves, whom I see now before me. Neither have I myself any real exis-tence, but am a shadow like the rest!"

"And how is it with your views of a future life?" in-quired the speculative clergyman.

"Worse than with you," said the old man, in a hollow and feeble tone; "for I cannot conceive it earnestly enough to feel either hope or fear. Mine--mine is the wretchedness! This cold heart--this unreal life! Ah! it grows colder still."

It so chanced, that at this juncture the decayed liga-ments of the skeleton gave way, and the dry bones fell together in a heap, thus causing the dusty wreath of cy-press to drop upon the table. The attention of the company being thus diverted, for a single instant, from Gervayse Hastings, they perceived, on turning again towards him, that the old man had undergone a change. His shadow had ceased to flicker on the wall.

"Well, Rosina, what is your criticism?" asked Roderick, as he rolled up the manuscript.

"Frankly, your success is by no means complete," re-plied she. "It is true, I have an idea of the character you endeavor to describe; but it is rather by dint of my own thought than your expression."

31

"That is unavoidable," observed the sculptor, "because the characteristics are all negative. If Gervayse Hastings could have imbibed one human grief at the gloomy banquet, the task of describing him would have been infinitely easier. Of such persons--and we do meet with these moral monsters now and then--it is difficult to conceive how they came to exist here, or what there is in them capable of existence hereafter. They seem to be on the outside of everything; and nothing wearies the soul more than an attempt to comprehend them within its grasp."

III   The Burglar's Christmas[1]
By Willa Cather

TWO very shabby looking young men stood at the corner of Prairie Avenue and Eightieth Street, looking despondently at the carriages that whirled by. It was Christmas Eve, and the streets were full of vehicles; florists' wagons, grocers' carts and carriages. The streets were in that half-liquid, half-congealed condition peculiar to the streets of Chicago at that season of the year. The swift wheels that spun by sometimes threw the slush of mud and snow over the two young men who were talking on the corner.

"Well," remarked the elder of the two, "I guess we are at our rope's end, sure enough. How do you feel?"

"Pretty shaky. The wind's sharp tonight. If I had had anything to eat I mightn't mind it so much. There is simply no show. I'm sick of the whole business. Looks like there's nothing for it but the lake."

"O, nonsense, I thought you had more grit. Got anything left you can hock?"

"Nothing but my beard, and Lam afraid they wouldn't find it worth a pawn ticket," said the younger man ruefully, rubbing the week's growth of stubble on his face.

"Got any folks anywhere? Now's your time to strike 'em if you have.

"Never mind if I have, they're out of the question."

"Well, you'll be out of it before many hours if you don't make a move of some sort. A man's got to eat. See here, I

[1] *This short story appeared above the signature of "Elizabeth L. Seymour" in the magazine Home Monthly, (December, 1896), VI, pp 8-10. At that time Cather had become the editor and was writing most of the issues.*

am going down to Longtin's saloon. I used to play the banjo in there with a couple of coons, and I'll bone him for some of his free-lunch stuff. You'd better come along, perhaps they'll fill an order for two."

"How far down is it?"

"Well, it's clear downtown, of course, 'way down on Michigan avenue.

"Thanks, I guess I'll loaf around here. I don't feel equal to the walk, and the cars--well, the cars are crowded." His features drew themselves into what might have been a smile under happier circumstances.

"No, you never did like street cars, you're too aristocratic. See here, Crawford, I don't like leaving you here. You ain't good company for yourself tonight."

"Crawford? O, yes, that's the last one. There have been so many I forget them."

"Have you got a real name, anyway?"

"O, yes, but it's one of the ones I've forgotten. Don't you worry about me. You go along and get your free lunch. I think I had a row in Longtin's place once. I'd better not show myself there again." As he spoke the young man nodded and turned slowly up the avenue.

He was miserable enough to want to be quite alone. Even the crowd that jostled by him annoyed him. He wanted to think about himself. He had avoided this final reckoning with himself for a year now. He had laughed it off and drunk it off. But now, when all those artificial devices which are employed to turn our thoughts into other channels and shield us from ourselves had failed him, it must come. Hunger is a powerful incentive to introspection.

It is a tragic hour, that hour when we are finally driven to reckon with ourselves, when every avenue of mental

distraction has been cut off and our own life and all its in-
effaceable failures closes about us like the walls of that old
torture chamber of the Inquisition. Tonight, as this man
stood stranded in the streets of the city, his hour came. It
was not the first time he had been hungry and desperate
and alone. But always before there had been some outlook,
some chance ahead, some pleasure yet untasted that
seemed worth the effort, some face that he fancied was, or
would be, dear. But it was not so tonight. The unyielding
conviction was upon him that he had failed in everything,
had outlived everything. It had been near him for a long
time, that Pale Spectre.

He had caught its shadow at the bottom of his glass
many a time, at the head of his bed when he was sleepless
at night, in the twilight shadows when some great sunset
broke upon him. It had made life hateful to him when he
awoke in the morning before now. But now it settled
slowly over him, like night, the endless Northern nights
that bid the sun a long farewell. It rose up before him like
granite. From this brilliant city with its glad bustle of Yule-
tide he was shut off as completely as though he were a
creature of another species. His days seemed numbered
and done, sealed over like the little coral cells at the bottom of the sea. Involuntarily he drew that cold air through
his lungs slowly, as though he were tasting it for the last
time.

Yet he was but four and twenty, this man--he looked
even younger--and he had a father some place down East
who had been very proud of him once. Well, he had taken
his life into his own hands, and this was what he had
made of it. That was all there was to be said. He could remember the hopeful things they used to say about him at
college in the old days, before he had cut away and begun

to live by his wits, and he found courage to smile at them now. They had read him wrongly. He knew now that he never had the essentials of success, only the superficial agility that is often mistaken for it. He was tow without the tinder, and he had burnt himself out at other people's fires. He had helped other people to make it win, but he himself--he had never touched an enterprise that had not failed eventually. Or, if it survived his connection with it, it left him behind.

His last venture had been with some ten-cent specialty company, a little lower than all the others, that had gone to pieces in Buffalo, and he had worked his way to Chicago by boat. When the boat made up its crew for the outward voyage, he was dispensed with as usual. He was used to that. The reason for it? O, there are so many reasons for failure! His was a very common one.

As he stood there in the wet under the street light he drew up his reckoning with the world and decided that it had treated him as well as he deserved. He had overdrawn his account once too often. There had been a day when he thought otherwise; when he had said he was unjustly handled, that his failure was merely the lack of proper ad-justment between himself and other men, that some day he would be recognized and it would all come right. But he knew better than that now, and he was still man enough to bear no grudge against any one--man or woman.

Tonight was his birthday, too. There seemed something particularly amusing in that. He turned up a limp little coat collar to try to keep a little of the wet chill from his throat, and instinctively began to remember all the birth-day parties he used to have. He was so cold and empty that his mind seemed unable to grapple with any serious question. He kept thinking about gingerbread and frosted cakes like a child. He could remember the splendid birthday parties his mother used to give him, when all the other little boys in the block came in their Sunday clothes and creaking shoes, with their ears still red from their mother's towel, and the pink and white birthday cake, and the stuffed olives and all the dishes of which he had been particularly fond, and how he would eat and eat and then go to bed and dream of Santa Claus. And in the morning he would awaken and eat again, until by night the family doctor arrived with his castor oil, and poor William used to dolefully say that it was altogether too much to have your birthday and Christmas all at once. He could remember, too, the royal birthday suppers he had given at college, and the stag dinners, and the toasts, and the music, and the good fellows who had wished him happiness and really meant what they said.

And since then there were other birthday suppers that he could not remember so clearly; the memory of them was heavy and flat, like cigarette smoke that has been shut in a room all night, like champagne that has been a day opened, a song that has been too often sung, an acute sensation that has been overstrained. They seemed tawdry and garish, discordant to him now. He rather wished he could forget them altogether.

Whichever way his mind now turned there was one thought that it could not escape, and that was the idea of food. He caught the scent of a cigar suddenly, and felt a sharp pain in the pit of his abdomen and a sudden moisture in his mouth. His cold hands clenched angrily, and for a moment he felt that bitter hatred of wealth, of ease, of everything that is well fed and well housed that is common to starving men. At any rate he had a right to eat! He had demanded great things from the world once: fame and wealth and admiration. Now it was simply bread-- and he would have it! He looked about him quickly and felt the blood begin to stir in his veins. In all his straits he had never stolen anything, his tastes were above it. But to-night thcre would be no tomorrow. He was amused at the way in which the idea excited him.

Was it possible there was yet one more experience that would distract him, one thing that had power to excite his jaded interest? Good! he had failed at everything else, now he would see what his chances would be as a common thief. It would be amusing to watch the beautiful consistency of his destiny work itself out even in that role. It would be interesting to add another study to his gallery of futile attempts, and then label them all: "the failure as a journalist," "the failure as a lecturer," "the failure as a business man," "the failure as a thief," and so on, like the titles under the pictures of the Dance of Death. It was time that Childe Roland came to the dark tower.

A girl hastened by him with her arms full of packages. She walked quickly and nervously, keeping well within the shadow, as if she were not accustomed to carrying bundles and did not care to meet any of her friends. As she crossed the muddy street, she made an effort to lift her skirt a little, and as she did so one of the packages slipped unnoticed from beneath her arm. He caught it up and overtook her. "Excuse me, but I think you dropped something."

She started, "O, yes, thank you, I would rather have lost anything than that."

The young man turned angrily upon himself. The package must have contained something of value. Why had he not kept it? Was this the sort of thief he would make? He

ground his teeth together. There is nothing more maddening than to have morally consented to crime and then lack
the nerve force to carry it out.

A carriage drove up to the house before which he stood.
Several richly dressed women alighted and went in. It was
a new house, and must have been built since he was in
Chicago last. The front door was open and he could see
down the hallway and up the staircase. The servant had
left the door and gone with the guests. The first floor was
brilliantly lighted, but the windows upstairs were dark. It
looked very easy, just to slip upstairs to the darkened
chambers where the jewels and trinkets of the fashionable
occupants were kept.

Still burning with impatience against himself he entered
quickly. Instinctively he removed his mud-stained hat as
he passed quickly and quietly up the stair case. It struck
him as being a rather superfluous courtesy in a burglar,
but he had done it before he had thought. His way was
clear enough, he met no one on the stairway or in the upper hall. The gas was lit in the upper hall. He passed the
first chamber door through sheer cowardice.

The second he entered quickly, thinking of something
else lest his courage should fail him, and closed the door
behind him. The light from the hall shone into the room
through the transom. The apartment was furnished richly
enough to justify his expectations. He went at once to the
dressing case. A number of rings and small trinkets lay in
a silver tray. These he put hastily in his pocket. He opened
the upper drawer and found, as he expected, several
leather cases. In the first he opened was a lady's watch, in
the second a pair of old-fashioned bracelets; he seemed to
dimly remember having seen bracelets like them before,
somewhere. The third case was heavier, the spring was

much worn, and it opened easily. It held a cup of some kind. He held it up to the light and then his strained nerves gave way and he uttered a sharp exclamation. It was the silver mug he used to drink from when he was a little boy.

The door opened, and a woman stood in the doorway facing him. She was a tall woman, with white hair, in evening dress. The light from the hall streamed in upon him, but she was not afraid. She stood looking at him a moment, then she threw out her hand and went quickly toward him.

"Willie, Willie! Is it you?"

He struggled to loose her arms from him, to keep her lips from his cheek. "Mother--you must not! You do not understand! O, my God, this is worst of all!" Hunger, weakness, cold, shame, all came back to him, and shook his self-control completely. Physically he was too weak to stand a shock like this. Why could it not have been an ordinary discovery, arrest, the station house and all the rest of it. Anything but this! A hard dry sob broke from him. Again he strove to disengage himself.

"Who is it says I shall not kiss my son? O, my boy, we have waited so long for this! You have been so long in coming, even I almost gave you up.

Her lips upon his cheek burnt him like fire. He put his hand to his throat, and spoke thickly and incoherently: "You do not understand. I did not know you were here. I came here to rob--it is the first time--I swear it--but I am a common thief. My pockets are full of your jewels now. Can't you hear me? I am a common thief!"

"Hush, my boy, those are ugly words. How could you rob your own house? How could you take what is your own? They are all yours, my son, as wholly yours as my great love--and you can't doubt that, Will, do you?"

That soft voice, the warmth and fragrance of her person stole through his chill, empty veins like a gentle stimulant. He felt as though all his strength were leaving him and even consciousness. He held fast to her and bowed his head on her strong shoulder, and groaned aloud.

"O, mother, life is hard, hard!"

She said nothing, but held him closer. And O, the strength of those white arms that held him! O, the assurance of safety in that warm bosom that rose and fell under his cheek! For a moment they stood so, silently. Then they heard a heavy step upon the stair. She led him to a chair and went out and closed the door. At the top of the stair-case she met a tall, broad-shouldered man, with iron gray hair, and a face alert and stern. Her eyes were shining and her cheeks on fire, her whole face was one expression of intense determination.

"James, it is William in there, come home. You must keep him at any cost. If he goes this time, I go with him. O, James, be easy with him, he has suffered so." She broke from a command to an entreaty, and laid her hand on his shoulder. He looked questioningly at her a moment, then went in the room and quietly shut the door.

She stood leaning against the wall, clasping her temples with her hands and listening to the low indistinct sound of the voices within. Her own lips moved silently. She waited a long time, scarcely breathing. At last the door opened, and her husband came out. He stopped to say in a shaken voice,

"You go to him now, he will stay. I will go to my room. I will see him again in the morning."

She put her arm about his neck, "O, James, I thank you, I thank you! This is the night he came so long ago, you re-

41

member? I gave him to you then, and now you give him back to me!"

"Don't, Helen," he muttered. "He is my son, I have never forgotten that. I failed with him. I don't like to fail, it cuts my pride. Take him and make a man of him." He passed on down the hall.

She flew into the room where the young man sat with his head bowed upon his knee. She dropped upon her knees beside him. Ah, it was so good to him to feel those arms again!

"He is so glad, Willie, so glad! He may not show it, but he is as happy as I. He never was demonstrative with either of us, you know."

"O, my God, he was good enough," groaned the man. "I told him everything, and he was good enough. I don't see how either of you can look at me, speak to me, touch me." He shivered under her clasp again as when she had first touched him, and tried weakly to throw her off. But she whispered softly, "This is my right, my son."

Presently, when he was calmer, she rose. "Now, come with me into the library, and I will have your dinner brought there."

As they went downstairs she remarked apologetically, "I will not call Ellen tonight; she has a number of guests to attend to. She is a big girl now, you know, and came out last winter. Besides, I want you all to myself tonight."

When the dinner came, and it came very soon, he fell upon it savagely. As he ate she told him all that had transpired during the years of his absence, and how his father's business had brought them there. "I was glad when we came. I thought you would drift West. I seemed a good deal nearer to you here."

There was a gentle unobtrusive sadness in her tone that

42

was too soft for a reproach.

"Have you everything you want? It is a comfort to see you eat."

He smiled grimly, "It is certainly a comfort to me. I have not indulged in this frivolous habit for some thirty-five hours."

She caught his hand and pressed it sharply, uttering a quick remonstrance.

"Don't say that! I know, but I can't hear you say it--it's too terrible! My boy, food has choked me many a time when I have thought of the possibility of that. Now take the old lounging chair by the fire, and if you are too tired to talk, we will just sit and rest together."

He sank into the depths of the big leather chair with the lions' heads on the arms, where he had sat so often in the days when his feet did not touch the floor and he was half afraid of the grim monsters cut in the polished wood. That chair seemed to speak to him of things long forgotten. It was like the touch of an old familiar friend. He felt a sudden yearning tenderness for the happy little boy who had sat there and dreamed of the big world so long ago. Alas, he had been dead many a summer, that little boy!

He sat looking up at the magnificent woman beside him. He had almost forgotten how handsome she was; how lustrous and sad were the eyes that were set under that serene brow, how impetuous and wayward the mouth even now, how superb the white throat and shoulders! Ah, the wit and grace and fineness of this woman!

He remembered how proud he had been of her as a boy when she came to see him at school. Then in the deep red coals of the grate he saw the faces of other women who had come since then into his vexed, disordered life. Laughing faces, with eyes artificially bright, eyes without depth

43

or meaning, features without the stamp of high sensibilities. And he had left this face for such as those!

He sighed restlessly and laid his hand on hers. There seemed refuge and protection in the touch of her, as in the old days when he was afraid of the dark. He had been in the dark so long now, his confidence was so thoroughly shaken, and he was bitterly afraid of the night and of himself.

"Ah, mother, you make other things seem so false. You must feel that I owe you an explanation, but I can't make any, even to myself. Ah, but we make poor exchanges in life. I can't make out the riddle of it all. Yet there are things I ought to tell you before I accept your confidence like this."

"I'd rather you wouldn't, Will. Listen: Between you and me there can be no secrets. We are more alike than other people. Dear boy, I know all about it. I am a woman, and circumstances were different with me, but we are of one blood. I have lived all your life before you. You have never had an impulse that I have not known, you have never touched a brink that my feet have not trod. This is your birthday night. Twenty-four years ago I foresaw all this. I was a young woman then and I had hot battles of my own, and I felt your likeness to me. You were not like other babies.

From the hour you were born you were restless and discontented, as I had been before you. You used to brace your strong little limbs against mine and try to throw me off as you did tonight. Tonight you have come back to me, just as you always did after you ran away to swim in the river that was forbidden you, the river you loved because it was forbidden. You are tired and sleepy, just as you used to be then, only a little older and a little paler and a little more foolish. I never asked you where you had been then, nor will I now. You have come back to me, that's all in all to me. I know your every possibility and limitation, as a composer knows his instrument."

He found no answer that was worthy to give to talk like this. He had not found life easy since he had lived by his wits. He had come to know poverty at close quarters. He had known what it was to be gay with an empty pocket, to wear violets in his buttonhole when he had not breakfasted, and all the hateful shams of the poverty of idleness.

He had been a reporter on a big metropolitan daily, where men grind out their brains on paper until they have not one idea left--and still grind on. He had worked in a real estate office, where ignorant men were swindled. He had sung in a comic opera chorus and played Harris in an Uncle Tom's Cabin company, and edited a socialist weekly. He had been dogged by debt and hunger and grinding poverty, until to sit here by a warm fire without concern as to how it would be paid for seemed unnatural.

He looked up at her questioningly. "I wonder if you know how much you pardon?"

"O, my poor boy, much or little, what does it matter? Have you wandered so far and paid such a bitter price for knowledge and not yet learned that love has nothing to do with pardon or forgiveness, that it only loves, and loves-- and loves? They have not taught you well, the women of your world." She leaned over and kissed him, as no woman had kissed him since he left her.

He drew a long sigh of rich content. The old life, with all its bitterness and useless antagonism and flimsy sophistries, its brief delights that were always tinged with fear and distrust and unfaith, that whole miserable, futile, swindled world of Bohemia seemed immeasurably distant and far away, like a dream that is over and done. And as the chimes rang joyfully outside and sleep pressed heavily upon his eyelids, he wondered dimly if the Author of this sad little riddle of ours were not able to solve it after all, and if the Potter would not finally mete out his all comprehensive justice, such as none but he could have, to his Things of Clay, which are made in his own patterns, weak or strong, for his own ends; and if some day we will not awaken and find that all evil is a dream, a mental distortion that will pass when the dawn shall break.

IV   A Chapparal Christmas Gift

By O. Henry[2]

The original cause of the trouble was about twenty years in growing. At the end of that time it was worth it.

Had you lived anywhere within fifty miles of Sundown Ranch you would have heard of it. It possessed a quantity of jet-black hair, a pair of extremely frank, deep-brown eyes, and a laugh that rippled across the prairie like the sound of a hidden brook. The name of it was Rosita McMullen; and she was the daughter of old man McMullen of the Sundown Sheep Ranch.

There came riding on red roan steeds--or, to be more explicit, on a paint and flea-bitten sorrel--two wooers. One was Madison Lane, and the other was the Frio Kid. But at that time they did not call him the Frio Kid, for he had not earned the honors of special nomenclature. His name was simply Johnny McRoy.

It must not be supposed that these two were the sum of the agreeable Rosita's admirers. The bronchos of a dozen others champed their bits at the long hitching rack of the Sundown Ranch. Many were the sheeps'-eyes that were cast in those savannas that did not belong to the flocks of Dan McMullen. But of all the cavaliers, Madison Lane and Johnny McRoy galloped far ahead, wherefore they are to be chronicled.

Madison Lane, a young cattleman from the Nueces country, won the race. He and Rosita were married one Christmas day. Armed, hilarious, vociferous, magnani-

[2] pen name of William Sidney Porter (1862-1910); this story appeared in the collection,Whirligigs, 1910

mous, the cowmen and the sheepmen, laying aside their hereditary hatred, joined forces to celebrate the occasion.

Sundown Ranch was sonorous with the cracking of jokes and six-shooters, the shine of buckles and bright eyes, the outspoken congratulations of the herders of kine.

But while the wedding feast was at its liveliest there descended upon it Johnny McRoy, bitten by jealousy, like one possessed.

"I'll give you a Christmas present," he yelled, shrilly, at the door, with his .45 in his hand. Even then he had some reputation as an offhand shot.

His first bullet cut a neat underbit in Madison Lane's right ear. The barrel of his gun moved an inch. The next shot would have been the bride's had not Carson, a sheepman, possessed a mind with triggers somewhat well oiled and in repair. The guns of the wedding party had been hung, in their belts, upon nails in the wall when they sat at table, as a concession to good taste. But Carson, with great promptness, hurled his plate of roast venison and frijoles at McRoy, spoiling his aim. The second bullet then, only shattered the white petals of a Spanish dagger flower suspended two feet above Rosita's head.

The guests spurned their chairs and jumped for their weapons. It was considered an improper act to shoot the bride and groom at a wedding. In about six seconds there were twenty or so bullets due to be whizzing in the direction of Mr. McRoy.

"I'll shoot better next time," yelled Johnny; "and there'll be a next time." He backed rapidly out of the door.

Carson, the sheepman, spurred on to attempt further exploits by the success of his plate throwing, was first to reach the door. McRoy's bullet from the darkness laid him low.

The cattlemen then swept out upon him, calling for vengeance, for, while the slaughter of a sheepman has not always lacked condonement, it was a decided misdemeanor in this instance. Carson was innocent; he was no accomplice at the matrimonial proceedings; nor had any one heard him quote the line "Christmas comes but once a year" to the guests.

But the sortie failed in its vengeance. McRoy was on his horse and away, shouting back curses and threats as he galloped into the concealing chaparral.

That night was the birthnight of the Frio Kid. He became the "bad man" of that portion of the State. The rejection of his suit by Miss McMullen turned him to a dangerous man. When officers went after him for the shooting of Carson, he killed two of them, and entered upon the life of an outlaw. He became a marvellous shot with either hand. He would turn up in towns and settlements, raise a quarrel at the slightest opportunity, pick off his man, and laugh at the officers of the law.

He was so cool, so deadly, so rapid, so inhumanly bloodthirsty that none but faint attempts were ever made to capture him. When he was at last shot and killed by a little one-armed Mexican who was nearly dead himself from fright, the Frio Kid had the deaths of eighteen men on his head. About half of these were killed in fair duels depending upon the quickness of the draw. The other half were men whom he assassinated from absolute wantonness and cruelty.

Many tales are told along the border of his impudent courage and daring. But he was not one of the breed of desperadoes who have seasons of generosity and even of softness. They say he never had mercy on the object of his anger. Yet at this and every Christmastide it is well to give each one credit, if it can be done, for whatever speck of good he may have possessed. If the Frio Kid ever did a kindly act or felt a throb of generosity in his heart it was once at such a time and season, and this is the way it happened.

One who has been crossed in love should never breathe the odor of the blossoms of the ratama tree. It stirs the memory to a dangerous degree.

One December in the Frio country there was a ratama tree in full bloom, for the winter had been as warm as springtime. That way rode the Frio Kid and his satellite and co-murderer, Mexican Frank. The kid reined in his mustang, and sat in his saddle, thoughtful and grim, with dangerously narrowing eyes. The rich, sweet scent touched him somewhere beneath his ice and iron.

"I don't know what I've been thinking about, Mex," he remarked in his usual mild draw, "to have forgot all about a Christmas present I got to give. I'm going to ride over to-morrow night and shoot Madison Lane in his own house. He got my girl--Rosita would have had me if he hadn't cut into the game. I wonder why I happened to overlook it up to now?"

"Ah, shucks, Kid," said Mexican, "don't talk foolishness. You know you can't get within a mile of Mad Lane's house to-morrow night. I see old man Allen day before yesterday, and he says Mad is going to have Christmas doings at his house. You remember how you shot up the festivities when Mad was married, and about the threats you made? Don't you suppose Mad Lane'll kind of keep his eye open for a certain Mr. Kid? You plumb make me tired, Kid, with such remarks."

"I'm going," repeated the Frio Kid, without heat, "to go to Madison Lane's Christmas doings, and kill him. I ought to have done it a long time ago. Why, Mex, just two weeks ago I dreamed me and Rosita was married instead of her and him; and we was living in a house, and I could see her smiling at me, and--oh! h--l, Mex, he got her; and I'll get him--yes, sir, on Christmas Eve he got her, and then's when I'll get him."

"There's other ways of committing suicide," advised Mexican. "Why don't you go and surrender to the sheriff?"

"I'll get him," said the Kid.

Christmas Eve fell as balmy as April. Perhaps there was a hint of faraway frostiness in the air, but it tingled like seltzer, perfumed faintly with late prairie blossoms and the mesquite grass.

When night came the five or six rooms of the ranch-house were brightly lit. In one room was a Christmas tree, for the Lanes had a boy of three, and a dozen or more guests were expected from the nearer ranches.

At nightfall Madison Lane called aside Jim Belcher and three other cowboys employed on his ranch.

"Now, boys," said Lane, "keep your eyes open. Walk around the house and watch the road well. All of you know the 'Frio Kid,' as they call him now, and if you see him, open fire on him without asking any questions. I'm not afraid of his coming around, but Rosita is. She's been afraid he'd come in on us every Christmas since we were married."

The guests had arrived in buckboards and on horse-back, and were making themselves comfortable inside.

The evening went along pleasantly. The guests enjoyed and praised Rosita's excellent supper, and afterward the men scattered in groups about the rooms or on the broad "gallery," smoking and chatting.

The Christmas tree, of course, delighted the youngsters,

and above all were they pleased when Santa Claus himself in magnificent white beard and furs appeared and began to distribute the toys.

"It's my papa," announced Billy Sampson, aged six. "I've seen him wear 'em before."

Berkly, a sheepman, an old friend of Lane, stopped Rosita as she was passing by him on the gallery, where he was sitting smoking.

"Well, Mrs. Lane," said he, "I suppose by this Christmas you've gotten over being afraid of that fellow McRoy, haven't you? Madison and I have talked about it, you know."

"Very nearly," said Rosita, smiling, "but I am still nervous sometimes. I shall never forget that awful time when he came so near to killing us."

"He's the most cold-hearted villain in the world," said Berkly. "The citizens all along the border ought to turn out and hunt him down like a wolf."

"He has committed awful crimes," said Rosita, "but--I--don't--know. I think there is a spot of good somewhere in everybody. He was not always bad--that I know."

Rosita turned into the hallway between the rooms. Santa Claus, in muffling whiskers and furs, was just coming through.

"I heard what you said through the window, Mrs. Lane," he said. "I was just going down in my pocket for a Christmas present for your husband. But I've left one for you, instead. It's in the room to your right."

"Oh, thank you, kind Santa Claus," said Rosita, brightly.

Rosita went into the room, while Santa Claus stepped into the cooler air of the yard.

She found no one in the room but Madison.

"Where is my present that Santa said he left for me in

here?" she asked. "Haven't seen anything in the way of a present," said her husband, laughing, "unless he could have meant me."

The next day Gabriel Radd, the foreman of the XO Ranch, dropped into the post-office at Loma Alta.

"Well, the Frio Kid's got his dose of lead at last," he remarked to the postmaster.

"That so? How'd it happen?"

"One of old Sanchez's Mexican sheep herders did it!-- think of it! the Frio Kid killed by a sheep herder! The Greaser saw him riding along past his camp about twelve o'clock last night, and was so skeered that he up with a Winchester and let him have it. Funniest part of it was that the Kid was dressed all up with white Angora-skin whiskers and a regular Santy Claus rig-out from head to foot. Think of the Frio Kid playing Santy!"

V To the Person Who Was Once a Child

You know, Beethoven's birthday comes just a little before Christmas. I heard on the radio that Beethoven was the best pianist of his day, but he didn't perform publicly until about age 28. Then he was said to play the piano so beautifully, with such expression and force, that his audience frequently wept. Whereupon the divine Beethoven rose from his stool and laughed. He said, 'Why do you cry? You are fools.' Well, I guess not all chefs are fat.

A week or so later that brings us to Christmas. Now, the professional writer faced with Christmas might well be filled with desperation. How can she write anything about such a hackneyed subject? True, the buying audience spends more money just before Christmas than at any other time of year. And magazines and newspapers are filled with commercial advertisements from merchants who need to sell off their stock, while the rest of the publication is starved for editorial content.

People want to read something genuine that makes them laugh or cry. But they don't really want to cry. Too childish. They buy books or recordings or other artifacts, often not so much to read them or learn from them or even enjoy them, but to express their cultural superiority, to show off their exquisite knowledge and attainment, by mere ownership and display of goods to prove they are worthy, and belong with the gods. Any real belly laughs, despair, or resemblance to the cold, cruel world is merely incidental. We are fools.

Many gods were never children. It might be a fact. But I prefer a god and a person who was once a child. The truth is, from my corner, life, and great art, often (or just some-times) do carry us away in spite of ourselves. Think of a great snow storm or the death of a child or parent. We think we are something, a respectable audience who has paid the price of admission. But we find we are once again in the helpless position of a infant in the middle of some-thing we cannot understand. All we can do is cry or laugh uncontrollably. Sorry, fools, no refunds.

This, child, is being human, this is life, this is great art. How can you be a reader, a writer, an artist, an ex-child, or a god without this experience?

Achieving this effect through art might be a trick that inspired artists can turn on when needed, without con-sciously knowing how. But I for one thank you, Beethoven, and I thank you, courageous writers and artists and people who take up tools for us fools, and communi-cate to us the truth of being human, just before Christmas, which is the story of a god who also was once a child.

You know, person who was once a child, if we listen carefully we might yet hear Him cry or laugh just as we did, and still do, cry and laugh once in a while. When we cry, the world cries. When we laugh, God laughs too, and He sometimes laughs at us when we are crying. We've paid our admission, why shouldn't we cry if we want to?

So cry on, deaf Beethoven! Laugh at us fools for joy! Merry Christmas, children of all ages!

VI Compliments of the Season
By O. Henry

There are no more Christmas stories to write. Fiction is exhausted; and newspaper items, the next best, are manufactured by clever young journalists who have married early and have an engagingly pessimistic view of life. Therefore, for seasonable diversion, we are reduced to two very questionable sources--facts and philosophy. We will begin with--whichever you choose to call it.

Children are pestilential little animals with which we have to cope under a bewildering variety of conditions. Especially when childish sorrows overwhelm them are we put to our wits' ends. We exhaust our paltry store of consolation; and then beat them, sobbing, to sleep. Then we grovel in the dust of a million years, and ask God why. Thus we call out of the rat-trap. As for the children, no one understands them except old maids, hunchbacks, and shepherd dogs.

Now come the facts in the case of the Rag-Doll, the Tatterdemalion, and the Twenty-fifth of December.

On the tenth of that month the Child of the Millionaire lost her rag-doll. There were many servants in the Millionaire's palace on the Hudson, and these ransacked the house and grounds, but without finding the lost treasure. The Child was a girl of five, and one of those perverse little beasts that often wound the sensibilities of wealthy parents by fixing their affections upon some vulgar, inexpensive toy instead of upon diamond-studded automobiles and pony phaetons.

The Child grieved sorely and truly, a thing inexplicable to the Millionaire, to whom the rag-doll market was about as interesting as Bay State Gas; and to the Lady, the Child's mother, who was all form--that is, nearly all, as you shall see.

The Child cried inconsolably, and grew hollow-eyed, knock-kneed, spindling, and cory-kilverty in many other respects. The Millionaire smiled and tapped his coffers confidently. The pick of the output of the French and German toymakers was rushed by special delivery to the mansion; but Rachel refused to be comforted. She was weeping for her rag child, and was for a high protective tariff against all foreign foolishness. Then doctors with the finest bedside manners and stop-watches were called in. One by one they chattered futilely about peptomanganate of iron and sea voyages and hypophosphites until their stop-watches showed that Bill Rendered was under the wire for show or place.

Then, as men, they advised that the rag-doll be found as soon as possible and restored to its mourning parent. The Child sniffed at therapeutics, chewed a thumb, and wailed for her Betsy. And all this time cablegrams were coming from Santa Claus saying that he would soon be here and enjoining us to show a true Christian spirit and let up on the poolrooms and tontine policies and platoon systems long enough to give him a welcome. Everywhere the spirit of Christmas was diffusing itself. The banks were refusing loans, the pawnbrokers had doubled their gang of helpers, people bumped your shins on the streets with red sleds, Thomas and Jeremiah bubbled before you on the bars while you waited on one foot, holly-wreaths of hospitality were hung in windows of the stores, they who had 'em were getting out their furs. You hardly knew which was the best bet in balls--three, high, moth, or snow. It was no time at which to lose the rag-doll of your heart.

If Doctor Watson's investigating friend had been called

in to solve this mysterious disappearance he might have observed on the Millionaire's wall a copy of "The Vampire." That would have quickly suggested, by induction, "A rag and a bone and a hank of hair." "Flip," a Scotch terrier, next to the rag-doll in the Child's heart, frisked through the halls. The hank of hair! Aha! X, the unfound quantity, represented the rag-doll. But, the bone? Well, when dogs find bones they--Done! it were an easy and a fruitful task to examine Flip's forefeet. Look, Watson! EarthÄdried earth between the toes. Of course, the dog--but Sherlock was not there. Therefore it devolves. But topography and architecture must intervene.

The Millionaire's palace occupied a lordly space. In front of it was a lawn close-mowed as a South Island man's face two days after a shave. At one side of it, and fronting on another street, was a pleasaunce trimmed to a leaf, and the garage and stables. The Scotch pup had ravished the rag-doll from the nursery, dragged it to a corner of the lawn, dug a hole, and buried it after the manner of careless undertakers. There you have the mystery solved, and no checks to write for the hypodermical wizard or fi'-pun notes to toss to the sergeant. Then let's get down to the heart of the thing, tiresome readers--the Christmas heart of the thing.

Fuzzy was drunk--not riotously or helplessly or loquaciously, as you or I might get, but decently, appropriately, and inoffensively, as becomes a gentleman down on his luck.

Fuzzy was a soldier of misfortune. The road, the haystack, the park bench, the kitchen door, the bitter round of eleemosynary beds-with-shower-bath-attachment, the petty pickings and ignobly garnered largesse of great cities--these formed the chapters of his history.

Fuzzy walked toward the river, down the street that bounded one side of the Millionaire's house and grounds. He saw a leg of Betsy, the lost rag-doll, protruding, like the clue to a Lilliputian murder mystery, from its untimely grave in a corner of the fence. He dragged forth the mal-treated infant, tucked it under his arm, and went on his way crooning a road song of his brethren that no doll that has been brought up to the sheltered life should hear. Well for Betsy that she had no ears. And well that she had no eyes save unseeing circles of black; for the faces of Fuzzy and the Scotch terrier were those of brothers, and the heart of no rag-doll could withstand twice to become the prey of such fearsome monsters.

Though you may never know it Grogan's saloon stands near the river and near the foot of the street down which Fuzzy traveled. In Grogan's, Christmas cheer was already rampant.

Fuzzy entered with his doll. He fancied that as a mum-mer at the feast of Saturn he might earn a few drops from the wassail cup.

He set Betsy on the bar and addressed her loudly and humorously, seasoning his speech with exaggerated com-pliments and endearments as one entertaining his lady friend. The loafers and bibbers around caught the farce of it, and roared. The bartender gave Fuzzy a drink. Oh, many of us carry rag-dolls.

"One for the lady?" suggested Fuzzy, impudently, and tucked another contribution to Art beneath his waistcoat.

He began to see possibilities in Betsy. His first-night had been a success. Visions of a vaudeville circuit about town dawned upon him.

In a group near the stove sat "Pigeon" McCarthy, Black Riley, and "One-ear" Mike, well and unfavorably known in the tough shoe-string district that blackened the left bank of the river. They passed a newspaper back and forth among themselves. The item that each solid and blunt forefinger pointed out was an advertisement headed "One Hundred Dollars Reward." To earn it one must return the rag-doll lost, strayed, or stolen from the Millionaire's mansion. It seemed that grief still ravaged, unchecked, in the bosom of the too faithful Child. Flip, the terrier, capered and shook his absurd whisker before her, powerless to distract. She wailed for her Betsy in the faces of walking, talking, mamaing, and eye-closing French Mabelles and Violettes. The advertisement was a last resort.

Black Riley came from behind the stove and approached Fuzzy in his one-sided parabolic way.

The Christmas mummer, flushed with success, had tucked Betsy under his arm, and was about to depart to the filling of impromptu dates elsewhere.

"Say, 'Bo," said Black Riley to him, "where did you cop out dat doll?"

"This doll?" asked Fuzzy, touching Betsy with his forefinger to be sure that she was the one referred to. "Why, this doll was presented to me by the Emperor of Beloochistan. I have seven hundred others in my country home in Newport. This doll--"

"Cheese the funny business," said Riley. "You swiped it or picked it up at de house on de hill where--but never mind dat. You want to take fifty cents for de rags, and take it quick. Me brother's kid at home might be wantin' to play wid it. Hey--what?"

He produced the coin.

Fuzzy laughed a gurgling, insolent, alcoholic laugh in his face. Go to the office of Sarah Bernhardt's manager and propose to him that she be released from a night's performance to entertain the Tackytown Lyceum and Literary Coterie. You will hear the duplicate of Fuzzy's laugh.

Black Riley gauged Fuzzy quickly with his blueberry eye as a wrestler does. His hand was itching to play the Roman and wrest the rag Sabine from the extemporaneous merry-andrew who was entertaining an angel unaware. But he refrained. Fuzzy was fat and solid and big. Three inches of well-nourished corporeity, defended from the winter winds by dingy linen, intervened between his vest and trousers. Countless small, circular wrinkles running around his coat-sleeves and knees guaranteed the quality of his bone and muscle. His small, blue eyes, bathed in the moisture of altruism and wooziness, looked upon you kindly, yet without abashment. He was whiskerly, whiskyly, fleshily formidable. So, Black Riley temporized.

"Wot'll you take for it, den?" he asked.

"Money," said Fuzzy, with husky firmness, "cannot buy her."

He was intoxicated with the artist's first sweet cup of attainment. To set a faded-blue, earth-stained rag-doll on a bar, to hold mimic converse with it, and to find his heart leaping with the sense of plaudits earned and his throat scorching with free libations poured in his honor--could base coin buy him from such achievements? You will perceive that Fuzzy had the temperament.

Fuzzy walked out with the gait of a trained sea-lion in search of other cafes to conquer.

Though the dusk of twilight was hardly yet apparent, lights were beginning to spangle the city like pop-corn bursting in a deep skillet. Christmas Eve, impatiently expected, was peeping over the brink of the hour. Millions had prepared for its celebration. Towns would be painted red. You, yourself, have heard the horns and dodged the capers of the Saturnalians.

"Pigeon" McCarthy, Black Riley, and "One-ear" Mike held a hasty converse outside Grogan's. They were narrow-chested, pallid striplings, not fighters in the open, but more dangerous in their ways of warfare than the most terrible of Turks. Fuzzy, in a pitched battle, could have eaten the three of them. In a go-as-you-please encounter he was already doomed.

They overtook him just as he and Betsy were entering Costigan's Casino. They deflected him, and shoved the newspaper under his nose. Fuzzy could read--and more.

"Boys," said he, "you are certainly damn true friends. Give me a week to think it over."

The soul of the real artist is quenched with difficulty.

The boys carefully pointed out to him that advertisements were soulless, and that the deficiencies of the day might not be supplied by the morrow.

"A cool hundred," said Fuzzy, thoughtfully and mushily.

"Boys," said he, "you are true friends. I'll go up and claim the reward. The show business is not what it used to be."

Night was falling more surely. The three tagged at his sides to the foot of the rise on which stood the Millionaire's house. There Fuzzy turned upon them acrimoniously.

"You are a pack of putty-faced beagle--hounds," he roared. "Go away."

They went away--a little way.

In "Pigeon" McCarthy's pocket was a section of one-inch gas-pipe eight inches long. In one end of it and in the middle of it was a lead slug. One-half of it was packed tight with solder. Black Riley carried a slung-shot, being a conventional thug. "One-ear" Mike relied upon a pair of brass knucks--an heirloom in the family.

"Why fetch and carry," said Black Riley, "when some one will do it for ye? Let him bring it out to us. Hey--what?"

"We can chuck him in the river," said "Pigeon" McCarthy, "with a stone tied to his feet."

"Youse guys make me tired," said "One-ear" Mike sadly. "Ain't progress ever appealed to none of yez? Sprinkle a little gasoline on 'em, and drop 'im on the Drive--well?"

Fuzzy entered the Millionaire's gate and zigzagged toward the softly glowing entrance of the mansion. The three goblins came up to the gate and lingered--one on each side of it, one beyond the roadway. They fingered their cold metal and leather, confident.

Fuzzy rang the door-bell, smiling foolishly and dreamily. An atavistic instinct prompted him to reach for the button of his right glove. But he wore no gloves; so his left hand dropped, embarrassed.

The particular menial whose duty it was to open doors to silks and laces shied at first sight of Fuzzy. But a second glance took in his passport, his card of admission, his surety of welcomeÄthe lost rag-doll of the daughter of the house dangling under his arm.

Fuzzy was admitted into a great hall, dim with the glow from unseen lights. The hireling went away and returned with a maid and the Child. The doll was restored to the mourning one. She clasped her lost darling to her breast; and then, with the inordinate selfishness and candor of childhood, stamped her foot and whined hatred and fear of the odious being who had rescued her from the depths of sorrow and despair. Fuzzy wriggled himself into an ingratiatory attitude and essayed the idiotic smile and blattering small talk that is supposed to charm the budding intellect of the young. The Child bawled, and was dragged away, hugging her Betsy close.

There came the Secretary, pale, poised, polished, gliding in pumps, and worshipping pomp and ceremony. He counted out into Fuzzy's hand ten ten-dollar bills; then dropped his eye upon the door, transferred it to James, its custodian, indicated the obnoxious earner of the reward with the other, and allowed his pumps to waft him away to secretarial regions.

James gathered Fuzzy with his own commanding optic and swept him as far as the front door.

When the money touched Fuzzy's dingy palm his first instinct was to take to his heels; but a second thought restrained him from that blunder of etiquette. It was his; it had been given him. It--and, oh, what an elysium it opened to the gaze of his mind's eye! He had tumbled to the foot of the ladder; he was hungry, homeless, friendless, ragged, cold, drifting; and he held in his hand the key to a paradise of the mud-honey that he craved. The fairy doll had waved a wand with her rag-stuffed hand; and now wherever he might go the enchanted palaces with shining foot-rests and magic red fluids in gleaming glassware would be open to him.

He followed James to the door.

He paused there as the flunky drew open the great mahogany portal for him to pass into the vestibule.

Beyond the wrought-iron gates in the dark highway Black Riley and his two pals casually strolled, fingering under their coats the inevitably fatal weapons that were to make the reward of the rag-doll theirs.

Fuzzy stopped at the Millionaire's door and bethought himself. Like little sprigs of mistletoe on a dead tree, certain living green thoughts and memories began to decorate his confused mind. He was quite drunk, mind you, and the present was beginning to fade. Those wreaths and festoons of holly with their scarlet berries making the great hall gay--where had he seen such things before? Somewhere he had known polished floors and odors of fresh flowers in winter, and--some one was singing a song in the house that he thought he had heard before. Some one singing and playing a harp. Of course, it was Christmas--Fuzzy thought he must have been pretty drunk to have overlooked that.

And then he went out of the present, and there came back to him out of some impossible, vanished, and irrevocable past a little, pure-white, transient, forgotten ghost-- the spirit of noblesse oblige. Upon a gentleman certain things devolve.

James opened the outer door. A stream of light went down the graveled walk to the iron gate. Black Riley, McCarthy, and "One-ear" Mike saw, and carelessly drew their sinister cordon closer about the gate.

With a more imperious gesture than James's master had ever used or could ever use, Fuzzy compelled the menial to close the door. Upon a gentleman certain things devolve. Especially at the Christmas season.

"It is cust--customary," he said to James, the flustered, "when a gentleman calls on Christmas Eve to pass the compliments of the season with the lady of the house. You und'stand? I shall not move shtep till I pass compl'ments season with lady the house. Und'stand?"

There was an argument. James lost. Fuzzy raised his voice and sent it through the house unpleasantly. I did not say he was a gentleman. He was simply a tramp being visited by a ghost.

A sterling silver bell rang. James went back to answer it,

leaving Fuzzy in the hall. James explained somewhere to some one.

Then he came and conducted Fuzzy to the library.

The Lady entered a moment later. She was more beautiful and holy than any picture that Fuzzy had seen. She smiled, and said something about a doll. Fuzzy didn't understand that; he remembered nothing about a doll.

A footman brought in two small glasses of sparkling wine on a stamped sterling-silver waiter. The Lady took one. The other was handed to Fuzzy.

As his fingers closed on the slender glass stem his disabilities dropped from him for one brief moment. He straightened himself; and Time, so disobliging to most of us, turned backward to accommodate Fuzzy.

Forgotten Christmas ghosts whiter than the false beards of the most opulent Kris Kringle were rising in the fumes of Grogan's whisky. What had the Millionaire's mansion to do with a long wainscoted Virginia hall, where the riders were grouped around a silver punch-bowl drinking the ancient toast of the House? And why should the patter of the cab horses' hoofs on the frozen street be in any wise related to the sound of the saddled hunters stamping under the shelter of the west veranda? And what had Fuzzy to do with any of it?

The Lady, looking at him over her glass, let her condescending smile fade away like a false dawn. Her eyes turned serious. She saw something beneath the rags and Scotch terrier whiskers that she did not understand. But it did not matter.

Fuzzy lifted his glass and smiled vacantly.

"P--pardon, lady," he said, "but couldn't leave without exchangin' comp'ments sheason with lady th' house. 'Gainst princ'ples gen'leman do sho."

And then he began the ancient salutation that was a tradition in the House when men wore lace ruffles and powder.

"The blessings of another year--"

Fuzzy's memory failed him. The Lady prompted:

"--Be upon this hearth."

"--The guest--" stammered Fuzzy.

"--And upon her who--quot; continued the Lady, with a leading smile. "Oh, cut it out," said Fuzzy, ill-manneredly. "I can't remember. Drink hearty."

Fuzzy had shot his arrow. They drank. The Lady smiled again the smile of her caste. James enveloped Fuzzy and re-conducted him toward the front door. The harp music still softly drifted through the house.

Outside, Black Riley breathed on his cold hands and hugged the gate. "I wonder," said the Lady to herself, musing, "who--but there were so many who came. I wonder whether memory is a curse or a blessing to them after they have fallen so low."

Fuzzy and his escort were nearly at the door. The Lady called: "James!"

James stalked back obsequiously, leaving Fuzzy waiting unsteadily, with his brief spark of the divine fire gone.

Outside, Black Riley stamped his cold feet and got a firmer grip on his section of gas-pipe.

"You will conduct this gentleman," said the Lady, "downstairs. Then tell Louis to get out the Mercedes and take him to whatever place he wishes to go."[3]

---

[3] his story appeared in the collection, Strictly Business, 1910

VII The Dead

By James Joyce

LILY, the caretaker's daughter, was literally run off her feet. Hardly had she brought one gentleman into the little pantry behind the office on the ground floor and helped him off with his overcoat, than the wheezy hall-door bell clanged again and she had to scamper along the bare hall-way to let in another guest. It was well for her she had not to attend to the ladies also. But Miss Kate and Miss Julia had thought of that and had converted the bathroom upstairs into a ladies' dressing-room. Miss Kate and Miss Julia were there, gossiping and laughing and fussing, walking after each other to the head of the stairs, peering down over the banisters and calling down to Lily to ask her who had come.

It was always a great affair, the Misses Morkan's annual dance. Everybody who knew them came to it, members of the family, old friends of the family, the members of Julia's choir, any of Kate's pupils that were grown up enough, and even some of Mary Jane's pupils too. Never once had it fallen flat. For years and years it had gone off in splen-did style, as long as anyone could remember: ever since Kate and Julia, after the death of their brother Pat, had left the house in Stoney Batter and taken Mary Jane, their only niece, to live with them in the dark, gaunt house on Usher's Island, the upper part of which they had rented from Mr Fulham, the corn-factor on the ground floor. That was a good thirty years ago if it was a day. Mary Jane, who was then a little girl in short clothes, was now the main prop of the household, for she had the organ in Haddington Road.

She had been through the Academy and gave a pupils'

concert every year in the upper room of the Ancient Concert Rooms. Many of her pupils belonged to the better-class families on the Kingstown and Dalkey line. Old as they were, her aunts also did their share. Julia, though she was quite grey, was still the leading soprano in Adam and Eve's, and Kate, being too feeble to go about much, gave music lessons to beginners on the old square piano in the back room. Lily, the caretaker's daughter, did housemaid's work for them. Though their life was modest, they believed in eating well; the best of everything: diamond-bone sirloins, three-shilling tea and the best bottled stout. But Lily seldom made a mistake in the orders, so that she got on well with her three mistresses. They were fussy, that was all. But the only thing they would not stand was back answers.

Of course, they had good reason to be fussy on such a night. And then it was long after ten o'clock and yet there was no sign of Gabriel and his wife. Besides they were dreadfully afraid that Freddy Malins might turn up screwed. They would not wish for worlds that any of Mary Jane's pupils should see him under the influence; and when he was like that it was sometimes very hard to manage him. Freddy Malins always came late, but they wondered what could be keeping Gabriel: and that was what brought them every two minutes to the banisters to ask Lily had Gabriel or Freddy come.

'O, Mr Conroy,' said Lily to Gabriel when she opened the door for him, 'Miss Kate and Miss Julia thought you were never coming. Good night, Mrs Conroy.'

'I'll engage they did,' said Gabriel, 'but they forget that my wife here takes three mortal hours to dress herself.'

He stood on the mat, scraping the snow from his goloshes, while Lily led his wife to the foot of the stairs and called out:

'Miss Kate, here's Mrs Conroy.'

Kate and Julia came toddling down the dark stairs at once. Both of them kissed Gabriel's wife, said she must be perished alive, and asked was Gabriel with her.

'Here I am as right as the mail, Aunt Kate! Go on up. I'll follow,' called out Gabriel from the dark.

He continued scraping his feet vigorously while the three women went upstairs, laughing, to the ladies' dressing-room. A light fringe of snow lay like a cape on the shoulders of his overcoat and like toecaps on the toes of his goloshes; and, as the buttons of his overcoat slipped with a squeaking noise through the snow-stiffened frieze, a cold, fragrant air from out-of-doors escaped from crevices and folds.

'Is it snowing again, Mr Conroy?' asked Lily.

She had preceded him into the pantry to help him off with his overcoat. Gabriel smiled at the three syllables she had given his surname and glanced at her. She was a slim, growing girl, pale in complexion and with hay-coloured hair. The gas in the pantry made her look still paler. Gabriel had known her when she was a child and used to sit on the lowest step nursing a rag doll.

'Yes, Lily,' he answered, 'and I think we're in for a night of it.'

He looked up at the pantry ceiling, which was shaking with the stamping and shuffling of feet on the floor above, listened for a moment to the piano and then glanced at the girl, who was folding his overcoat carefully at the end of a shelf.

'Tell me, Lily,' he said in a friendly tone, 'do you still go to school?'

'O no, sir,' she answered. 'I'm done schooling this year

70

and more.'

'O, then,' said Gabriel gaily, 'I suppose we'll be going to your wedding one of these fine days with your young man, eh?'

The girl glanced back at him over her shoulder and said with great bitterness:

'The men that is now is only all palaver and what they can get out of you.'

Gabriel coloured, as if he felt he had made a mistake, and, without looking at her, kicked off his goloshes and flicked actively with his muffler at his patent-leather shoes.

He was a stout, tallish young man. The high colour of his cheeks pushed upwards even to his forehead, where it scattered itself in a few formless patches of pale red; and on his hairless face there scintillated restlessly the polished lenses and the bright gilt rims of the glasses which screened his delicate and restless eyes. His glossy black hair was parted in the middle and brushed in a long curve behind his ears where it curled slightly beneath the groove left by his hat.

When he had flicked lustre into his shoes he stood up and pulled his waistcoat down more tightly on his plump body. Then he took a coin rapidly from his pocket.

'O Lily,' he said, thrusting it into her hands, 'it's Christmastime, isn't it? Just... here's a little... '

He walked rapidly towards the door.

'O no, sir!' cried the girl, following him. 'Really, sir, I wouldn't take it.'

'Christmas-time! Christmas-time!' said Gabriel, almost trotting to the stairs and waving his hand to her in deprecation.

The girl, seeing that he had gained the stairs, called out

after him:

'Well, thank you, sir.'

He waited outside the drawing-room door until the waltz should finish, listening to the skirts that swept against it and to the shuffling of feet. He was still discomposed by the girl's bitter and sudden retort. It had cast a gloom over him which he tried to dispel by arranging his cuffs and the bows of his tie. He then took from his waistcoat pocket a little paper and glanced at the headings he had made for his speech. He was undecided about the lines from Robert Browning, for he feared they would be above the heads of his hearers. Some quotation that they would recognize from Shakespeare or from the Melodies would be better. The indelicate clacking of the men's heels and the shuffling of their soles reminded him that their grade of culture differed from his. He would only make himself ridiculous by quoting poetry to them which they could not understand. They would think that he was airing his superior education. He would fail with them just as he had failed with the girl in the pantry. He had taken up a wrong tone. His whole speech was a mistake from first to last, an utter failure.

Just then his aunts and his wife came out of the ladies' dressing-room. His aunts were two small, plainly dressed old women. Aunt Julia was an inch or so the taller. Her hair, drawn low over the tops of her ears, was grey; and grey also, with darker shadows, was her large flaccid face. Though she was stout in build and stood erect, her slow eyes and parted lips gave her the appearance of a woman who did not know where she was or where she was going. Aunt Kate was more vivacious. Her face, healthier than her sister's, was all puckers and creases, like a shrivelled red apple, and her hair, braided in the same old-fashioned way, had not lost its ripe nut colour.

They both kissed Gabriel frankly. He was their favourite nephew, the son of their dead elder sister, Ellen, who had married T. J. Conroy of the Port and Docks.

'Gretta tells me you're not going to take a cab back to Monkstown tonight, Gabriel,' said Aunt Kate.

'No,' said Gabriel, turning to his wife, 'we had quite enough of that last year, hadn't we? Don't you remember, Aunt Kate, what a cold Gretta got out of it? Cab windows rattling all the way, and the east wind blowing in after we passed Merrion. Very jolly it was. Gretta caught a dreadful cold.'

Aunt Kate frowned severely and nodded her head at every word.

'Quite right, Gabriel, quite right,' she said. 'You can't be too careful.'

'But as for Gretta there,' said Gabriel, 'she'd walk home in the snow if she were let.'

Mrs Conroy laughed.

'Don't mind him, Aunt Kate,' she said. 'He's really an awful bother, what with green shades for Tom's eyes at night and making him do the dumb-bells, and forcing Eva to eat the stirabout. The poor child! And she simply hates the sight of it!... O, but you'll never guess what he makes me wear now!'

She broke out into a peal of laughter and glanced at her husband, whose admiring and happy eyes had been wandering from her dress to her face and hair. The two aunts laughed heartily, too, for Gabriel's solicitude was a standing joke with them.

'Goloshes!' said Mrs Conroy. 'That's the latest. Whenever it's wet underfoot I must put on my goloshes. Tonight even, he wanted me to put them on, but I wouldn't. The next thing he'll buy me will be a diving suit.'

Gabriel laughed nervously and patted his tie reassuringly, while Aunt Kate nearly doubled herself, so heartily did she enjoy the joke. The smile soon faded from Aunt Julia's face and her mirthless eyes were directed towards her nephew's face. After a pause she asked:

'And what are goloshes, Gabriel?'

'Goloshes, Julia!' exclaimed her sister. 'Goodness me, don't you know what goloshes are? You wear them over your... over your boots, Gretta, isn't it?'

'Yes,' said Mrs Conroy. 'Gutta-percha things. We both have a pair now. Gabriel says everyone wears them on the Continent.'

'O, on the Continent,' murmured Aunt Julia, nodding her head slowly.

Gabriel knitted his brows and said, as if he were slightly angered:

'It's nothing very wonderful, but Gretta thinks it very funny, because she says the word reminds her of Christy Minstrels.'

'But tell me, Gabriel,' said Aunt Kate, with brisk tact. 'Of course, you've seen about the room. Gretta was saying... '

'O, the room is all right,' replied Gabriel. 'I've taken one in the Gresham.'

'To be sure,' said Aunt Kate, 'by far the best thing to do. And the children, Gretta, you're not anxious about them?'

'O, for one night,' said Mrs Conroy. 'Besides, Bessie will look after them.'

'To be sure,' said Aunt Kate again. 'What a comfort it is to have a girl like that, one you can depend on! There's that Lily, I'm sure I don't know what has come over her lately. She's not the girl she was at all.'

Gabriel was about to ask his aunt some questions on

this point, but she broke off suddenly to gaze after her sister, who had wandered down the stairs and was craning her neck over the banisters.

'Now, I ask you,'she said almost testily, 'where is Julia going? Julia! Julia! Where are you going?'

Julia, who had gone half-way down one flight, came back and announced blandly:

'Here's Freddy.'

At the same moment a clapping of hands and a final flourish of the pianist told that the waltz had ended. The drawing-room door was opened from within and some couples came out. Aunt Kate drew Gabriel aside hurriedly and whispered into his ear:

'Slip down, Gabriel, like a good fellow and see if he's all right, and don't let him up if he's screwed. I'm sure he's screwed. I'm sure he is.'

Gabriel went to the stairs and listened over the banisters. He could hear two persons talking in the pantry. Then he recognized Freddy Malins' laugh. He went down the stairs noisily.

'It's such a relief,' said Aunt Kate to Mrs Conroy, 'that Gabriel is here. I always feel easier in my mind when he's here... Julia, there's Miss Daly and Miss Power will take some refreshment. Thanks for your beautiful waltz, Miss Daly. It made lovely time.'

A tall wizen-faced man, with a stiff grizzled moustache and swarthy skin, who was passing out with his partner, said:

'And may we have some refreshment, too, Miss Morkan?'

'Julia,' said Aunt Kate summarily, 'and here's Mr Browne and Miss Furlong. Take them in, Julia, with Miss Daly and Miss Power.'

'I'm the man for the ladies,' said Mr Browne, pursing his lips until his moustache bristled, and smiling in all his wrinkles. 'You know, Miss Morkan, the reason they are so fond of me is--'

He did not finish his sentence, but, seeing that Aunt Kate was out of earshot, at once led the three young ladies into the back room. The middle of the room was occupied by two square tables placed end to end, and on these Aunt Julia and the caretaker were straightening and smoothing a large cloth. On the sideboard were arrayed dishes and plates, and glasses and bundles of knives and forks and spoons. The top of the closed square piano served also as a sideboard for viands and sweets. At a smaller sideboard in one corner two young men were standing, drinking hop-bitters.

Mr Browne led his charges thither and invited them all, in jest, to some ladies' punch, hot, strong, and sweet. As they said they never took anything strong, he opened three bottles of lemonade for them. Then he asked one of the young men to move aside, and, taking hold of the de-canter, filled out for himself a goodly measure of whisky. The young men eyed him respectfully while he took a trial sip.

'God help me,' he said, smiling, 'it's the doctor's order.'

His wizened face broke into a broader smile, and the three young ladies laughed in musical echo to his pleas-antry, swaying their bodies to and fro, with nervous jerks of their shoulders. The boldest said:

'O, now, Mr Browne, I'm sure the doctor never ordered anything of the kind.'

Mr Browne took another sip of his whisky and said, with sidling mimicry:

'Well, you see, I'm the famous Mrs Cassidy, who is reported to have said: "Now, Mary Grimes, if I don't take it, make me take it, for I feel I want it."'

His hot face had leaned forward a little too confidentially and he had assumed a very low Dublin accent, so that the young ladies, with one instinct, received his speech in silence. Miss Furlong, who was one of Mary Jane's pupils, asked Miss Daly what was the name of the pretty waltz she had played; and Mr Browne, seeing that he was ignored, turned promptly to the two young men, who were more appreciative.

A red-faced young woman, dressed in pansy, came into the room, excitedly clapping her hands and crying:

'Quadrilles! Quadrilles!'

Close on her heels came Aunt Kate, crying:

'Two gentlemen and three ladies, Mary Jane!'

'O, here's Mr Bergin and Mr Kerrigan,' said Mary Jane. 'Mr Kerrigan, will you take Miss Power? Miss Furlong, may I get you a partner, Mr Bergin. O, that'll just do now.'

'Three ladies, Mary Jane,' said Aunt Kate.

The two young gentlemen asked the ladies if they might have the pleasure, and Mary Jane turned to Miss Daly.

'O, Miss Daly, you're really awfully good, after playing for the last two dances, but really we're so short of ladies tonight.'

'I don't mind in the least, Miss Morkan.'

'But I've a nice partner for you, Mr Bartell D'Arcy, the tenor. I'll get him to sing later on. All Dublin is raving about him.'

'Lovely voice, lovely voice!' said Aunt Kate.

As the piano had twice begun the prelude to the first figure Mary Jane led her recruits quickly from the room. They had hardly gone when Aunt Julia wandered slowly into the room, looking behind her at something.

'What is the matter, Julia?' asked Aunt Kate anxiously. 'Who is it?'

Julia, who was carrying in a column of table-napkins, turned to her sister and said, simply, as if the question had surprised her:

'It's only Freddy, Kate, and Gabriel with him.'

In fact, right behind her Gabriel could be seen piloting Freddy Malins across the landing. The latter, a young man of about forty, was of Gabriel's size and build, with very round shoulders. His face was fleshy and pallid, touched with colour only at the thick hanging lobes of his ears and at the wide wings of his nose. He had coarse features, a blunt nose, a convex and receding brow, tumid and pro-truded lips. His heavy-lidded eyes and the disorder of his scanty hair made him look sleepy. He was laughing heart-ily in a high key at a story which he had been telling Gabriel on the stairs and at the same time rubbing the knuckles of his left fist backwards and forwards into his left eye.

'Good evening, Freddy,' said Aunt Julia.

Freddy Malins bade the Misses Morkan good evening in what seemed an off-hand fashion by reason of the ha-bitual catch in his voice and then, seeing that Mr Browne was grinning at him from the sideboard, crossed the room on rather shaky legs and began to repeat in an undertone the story he had just told to Gabriel.

'He's not so bad, is he?' said Aunt Kate to Gabriel.

Gabriel's brows were dark, but he raised them quickly and answered:

'O, no, hardly noticeable.'

'Now, isn't he a terrible fellow!' she said. 'And his poor mother made him take the pledge on New Year's Eve. But come on, Gabriel, into the drawing-room.'

Before leaving the room with Gabriel she signalled to Mr Browne by frowning and shaking her forefinger in warning to and fro. Mr Browne nodded in answer and, when she had gone, said to Freddy Malins:

'Now, then, Teddy, I'm going to fill you out a good glass of lemonade just to buck you up.'

Freddy Malins, who was nearing the climax of his story, waved the offer aside impatiently, but Mr Browne, having first called Freddy Malins' attention to a disarray in his dress, filled out and handed him a full glass of lemonade. Freddy Malins' left hand accepted the glass mechanically, his right hand being engaged in the mechanical readjustment of his dress. Mr Browne, whose face was once more wrinkling with mirth, poured out for himself a glass of whisky while Freddy Malins exploded, before he had well reached the climax of his story, in a kink of high-pitched bronchitic laughter and, setting down his untasted and overflowing glass, began to run the knuckles of his left fist backwards and forwards into his left eye, repeating words of his last phrase as well as his fit of laughter would allow him.

Gabriel could not listen while Mary Jane was playing her Academy piece, full of runs and difficult passages, to the hushed drawing-room. He liked music, but the piece she was playing had no melody for him and he doubted whether it had any melody for the other listeners, though they had begged Mary Jane to play something. Four young men, who had come from the refreshment-room to stand in the doorway at the sound of the piano, had gone away quietly in couples after a few minutes. The only persons who seemed to follow the music were Mary Jane herself, her hands racing along the keyboard or lifted from it at the pauses like those of a priestess in momentary imprecation, and Aunt Kate standing at her elbow to turn the page.

Gabriel's eyes, irritated by the floor, which glittered with beeswax under the heavy chandelier, wandered to the wall above the piano. A picture of the balcony scene in Romeo and Juliet hung there and beside it was a picture of the two murdered princes in the Tower which Aunt Julia had worked in red, blue, and brown wools when she was a girl. Probably in the school they had gone to as girls that kind of work had been taught for one year. His mother had worked for him as a birthday present a waist-coat of purple tabinet, with little foxes' heads upon it, lined with brown satin and having round mulberry buttons. It was strange that his mother had had no musical talent, though Aunt Kate used to call her the brains carrier of the Morkan family.

Both she and Julia had always seemed a little proud of their serious and matronly sister. Her photograph stood before the pier-glass. She had an open book on her knees and was pointing out something in it to Constantine who, dressed in a man-o'-war suit, lay at her feet. It was she who had chosen the names of her sons, for she was very sensible of the dignity of family life. Thanks to her, Constantine was now senior curate in Balbriggan and, thanks to her, Gabriel himself had taken his degree in the Royal University. A shadow passed over his face as he remembered her sullen opposition to his marriage. Some slighting phrases she had used still rankled in his memory; once she had spoken of Gretta as being country cute and that was not true of Gretta at all. It was Gretta who had nursed her during all her last long illness in their house at Monkstown.

He knew that Mary Jane must be near the end of her

piece, for she was playing again the opening melody with runs of scales after every bar, and while he waited for the end the resentment died down in his heart. The piece ended with a trill of octaves in the treble and a final deep octave in the bass. Great applause greeted Mary Jane as, blushing and rolling up her music nervously, she escaped from the room. The most vigorous clapping came from the four young men in the doorway who had gone away to the refreshment-room at the beginning of the piece but had come back when the piano had stopped.

Lancers were arranged. Gabriel found himself part-nered with Miss Ivors. She was a frank-mannered, talkative young lady, with a freckled face and prominent brown eyes. She did not wear a low-cut bodice, and the large brooch which was fixed in the front of her collar bore on it an Irish device and motto.

When they had taken their places she said abruptly:

'I have a crow to pluck with you.'

'With me?' said Gabriel.

She nodded her head gravely.

'What is it?' asked Gabriel, smiling at her solemn man-ner.

'Who is G.C.?' answered Miss Ivors, turning her eyes upon him.

Gabriel coloured and was about to knit his brows, as if he did not understand, when she said bluntly:

'O, innocent Amy! I have found out that you write for The Daily Express. Now, aren't you ashamed of your-self?'

'Why should I be ashamed of myself?' asked Gabriel, blinking his eyes and trying to smile.

'Well, I'm ashamed of you,' said Miss Ivors frankly. 'To say you'd write for a paper like that. I didn't think you were a West Briton.'

A look of perplexity appeared on Gabriel's face. It was true that he wrote a literary column every Wednesday in The Daily Express, for which he was paid fifteen shillings. But that did not make him a West Briton surely. The books he received for review were almost more welcome than the paltry cheque. He loved to feel the covers and turn over the pages of newly printed books. Nearly every day when his teaching in the college was ended he used to wander down the quays to the second-hand booksellers, to Hickey's on Bachelor's Walk, to Webb's or Massey's on Aston's Quay, or to O'Clohissey's in the by-street. He did not know how to meet her charge. He wanted to say that literature was above politics. But they were friends of many years' standing and their careers had been parallel, first at the University and then as teachers: he could not risk a grandiose phrase with her. He continued blinking his eyes and trying to smile and murmured lamely that he saw nothing political in writing reviews of books.

When their turn to cross had come he was still perplexed and inattentive. Miss Ivors promptly took his hand in a warm grasp and said in a soft friendly tone:

'Of course, I was only joking. Come, we cross now.'

When they were together again she spoke of the University question and Gabriel felt more at ease. A friend of hers had shown her his review of Browning's poems. That was how she had found out the secret: but she liked the review immensely.

Then she said suddenly:

'O, Mr Conroy, will you come for an excursion to the Aran Isles this summer? We're going to stay there a whole month. It will be splendid out in the Atlantic. You ought to come. Mr Clancy is coming, and Mr Kilkelly and Kathleen

Kearney. It would be splendid for Gretta too if she'd come. She's from Connacht, isn't she?'

'Her people are,' said Gabriel shortly.

'But you will come, won't you?' said Miss Ivors, laying her warm hand eagerly on his arm.

'The fact is,' said Gabriel, 'I have just arranged to go--'

'Go where?' asked Miss Ivors.

'Well, you know, every year I go for a cycling tour with some fellows and so--'

'But where?' asked Miss Ivors.

'Well, we usually go to France or Belgium or perhaps Germany,' said Gabriel awkwardly.

'And why do you go to France and Belgium,' said Miss Ivors, 'instead of visiting your own land?'

'Well,' said Gabriel, 'it's partly to keep in touch with the languages and partly for a change.'

'And haven't you your own language to keep in touch with--Irish?' asked Miss Ivors.

'Well,' said Gabriel, 'if it comes to that, you know, Irish is not my language.'

Their neighbours had turned to listen to the cross-examination. Gabriel glanced right and left nervously and tried to keep his good humour under the ordeal, which was making a blush invade his forehead.

'And haven't you your own land to visit,' continued Miss Ivors, 'that you know nothing of, your own people, and your own country?'

'O, to tell you the truth,' retorted Gabriel suddenly, 'I'm sick of my own country, sick of it!'

'Why?' asked Miss Ivors.

Gabriel did not answer, for his retort had heated him.

'Why?' repeated Miss Ivors.

They had to go visiting together and, as he had not answered her, Miss Ivors said warmly:

'Of course, you've no answer.'

Gabriel tried to cover his agitation by taking part in the dance with great energy. He avoided her eyes, for he had seen a sour expression on her face. But when they met in the long chain he was surprised to feel his hand firmly pressed. She looked at him from under her brows for a moment quizzically until he smiled. Then, just as the chain was about to start again, she stood on tiptoe and whispered into his ear:

'West Briton!'

When the lancers were over Gabriel went away to a remote corner of the room where Freddy Malins' mother was sitting. She was a stout, feeble old woman with white hair. Her voice had a catch in it like her son's and she stuttered slightly. She had been told that Freddy had come and that he was nearly all right. Gabriel asked her whether she had had a good crossing. She lived with her married daughter in Glasgow and came to Dublin on a visit once a year. She answered placidly that she had had a beautiful crossing and that the captain had been most attentive to her. She spoke also of the beautiful house her daughter kept in Glasgow, and of all the friends they had there. While her tongue rambled on Gabriel tried to banish from his mind all memory of the unpleasant incident with Miss Ivors. Of course the girl, or woman, or whatever she was, was an enthusiast, but there was a time for all things. Perhaps he ought not to have answered her like that. But she had no right to call him a West Briton before people, even in joke. She had tried to make him ridiculous before people, heckling him and staring at him with her rabbit's eyes.

He saw his wife making her way towards him through the waltzing couples. When she reached him she said into his ear:

'Gabriel, Aunt Kate wants to know won't you carve the goose as usual. Miss Daly will carve the ham and I'll do the pudding.'

'All right,' said Gabriel.

'She's sending in the younger ones first as soon as this waltz is over so that we'll have the table to ourselves.'

'Were you dancing?' asked Gabriel.

'Of course I was. Didn't you see me? What row had you with Molly Ivors?'

'No row. Why? Did she say so?'

'Something like that. I'm trying to get that Mr D'Arcy to sing. He's full of conceit, I think.'

'There was no row,' said Gabriel moodily, 'only she wanted me to go for a trip to the west of Ireland and I said I wouldn't.'

His wife clasped her hands excitedly and gave a little jump.

'O, do go, Gabriel,' she cried. 'I'd love to see Galway again.'

'You can go if you like,' said Gabriel coldly.

She looked at him for a moment, then turned to Mrs Malins and said:

'There's a nice husband for you, Mrs Malins.'

While she was threading her way back across the room Mrs Malins, without adverting to the interruption, went on to tell Gabriel what beautiful places there were in Scotland and beautiful scenery. Her son-in-law brought them every year to the lakes and they used to go fishing. Her son-in-law was a splendid fisher. One day he caught a beautiful big fish and the man in the hotel cooked it for their dinner.

Gabriel hardly heard what she said. Now that supper

was coming near he began to think again about his speech and about the quotation. When he saw Freddy Malins coming across the room to visit his mother Gabriel left the chair free for him and retired into the embrasure of the window. The room had already cleared and from the back room came the clatter of plates and knives. Those who still remained in the drawing-room seemed tired of dancing and were conversing quietly in little groups. Gabriel's warm, trembling fingers tapped the cold pane of the window. How cool it must be outside! How pleasant it would be to walk out alone, first along by the river and then through the park! The snow would be lying on the branches of the trees and forming a bright cap on the top of the Wellington Monument. How much more pleasant it would be there than at the supper-table!

He ran over the headings of his speech: Irish hospitality, sad memories, the Three Graces, Paris, the quotation from Browning. He repeated to himself a phrase he had written in his review: 'One feels that one is listening to a thought-tormented music.' Miss Ivors had praised the review. Was she sincere? Had she really any life of her own behind all her propagandism? There had never been any ill-feeling between them until that night. It unnerved him to think that she would be at the supper-table, looking up at him, while he spoke, with her critical quizzing eyes. Perhaps she would not be sorry to see him fail in his speech. An idea came into his mind and gave him courage.

He would say, alluding to Aunt Kate and Aunt Julia: 'Ladies and Gentlemen, the generation which is now on the wane among us may have had its faults, but for my part I think it had certain qualities of hospitality, of humour, of humanity, which the new and very serious and hyper-educated generation that is growing up around us seems to me to lack.' Very good: that was one for Miss Ivors. What did he care that his aunts were only two ignorant old women?

A murmur in the room attracted his attention. Mr Browne was advancing from the door, gallantly escorting Aunt Julia, who leaned upon his arm, smiling and hanging her head. An irregular musketry of applause escorted her also as far as the piano and then, as Mary Jane seated herself on the stool, and Aunt Julia, no longer smiling, half turned so as to pitch her voice fairly into the room, gradually ceased. Gabriel recognized the prelude. It was that of an old song of Aunt Julia's--'Arrayed for the Bridal'. Her voice, strong and clear in tone, attacked with great spirit the runs which embellish the air, and though she sang very rapidly she did not miss even the smallest of the grace notes. To follow the voice, without looking at the singer's face, was to feel and share the excitement of swift and secure flight. Gabriel applauded loudly with all the others at the close of the song, and loud applause was borne in from the invisible supper-table.

It sounded so genuine that a little colour struggled into Aunt Julia's face as she bent to replace in the music-stand the old leather-bound song-book that had her initials on the cover. Freddy Malins, who had listened with his head perched sideways to hear her better, was still applauding when everyone else had ceased and talking animatedly to his mother, who nodded her head gravely and slowly in acquiescence. At last, when he could clap no more, he stood up suddenly and hurried across the room to Aunt Julia whose hand he seized and held in both his hands, shaking it when words failed him or the catch in his voice proved too much for him.

'I was just telling my mother,' he said, 'I never heard

you sing so well, never. No, I never heard your voice so good as it is tonight. Now! Would you believe that now? That's the truth. Upon my word and honour that's the truth. I never heard your voice sound so fresh and so... so clear and fresh, never.'

Aunt Julia smiled broadly and murmured something about compliments as she released her hand from his grasp. Mr Browne extended his open hand towards her and said to those who were near him in the manner of a showman introducing a prodigy to an audience:

'Miss Julia Morkan, my latest discovery!'

He was laughing very heartily at this himself when Freddy Malins turned to him and said:

'Well, Browne, if you're serious you might make a worse discovery. All I can say is I never heard her sing half so well as long as I am coming here. And that's the honest truth.'

'Neither did I,' said Mr Browne. 'I think her voice has greatly improved.'

Aunt Julia shrugged her shoulders and said with meek pride:

'Thirty years ago I hadn't a bad voice as voices go.'

'I often told Julia,' said Aunt Kate emphatically, 'that she was simply thrown away in that choir. But she never would be said by me.'

She turned as if to appeal to the good sense of the others against a refractory child, while Aunt Julia gazed in front of her, a vague smile of reminiscence playing on her face.

'No,' continued Aunt Kate, 'she wouldn't be said or led by anyone, slaving there in that choir night and day, night and day. Six o'clock on Christmas morning! And all for what?'

'Well, isn't it for the honour of God, Aunt Kate?' asked

Mary Jane, twisting round on the piano-stool and smiling.

Aunt Kate turned fiercely on her niece and said:

'I know all about the honour of God, Mary Jane, but I think it's not at all honourable for the Pope to turn out the women out of the choirs that have slaved there all their lives and put little whipper-snappers of boys over their heads. I suppose it is for the good of the Church, if the Pope does it. But it's not just, Mary Jane, and it's not right.'

She had worked herself into a passion and would have continued in defence of her sister, for it was a sore subject with her, but Mary Jane, seeing that all the dancers had come back, intervened pacifically.

'Now, Aunt Kate, you're giving scandal to Mr Browne, who is of the other persuasion.'

Aunt Kate turned to Mr Browne, who was grinning at this allusion to his religion, and said hastily:

'O, I don't question the Pope's being right. I'm only a stupid old woman and I wouldn't presume to do such a thing. But there's such a thing as common everyday politeness and gratitude. And if I were in Julia's place I'd tell that Father Healey straight up to his face...'

'And besides, Aunt Kate,' said Mary Jane, 'we really are all hungry and when we are hungry we are all very quarrelsome.'

'And when we are thirsty we are also quarrelsome,' added Mr Browne.

'So that we had better go to supper,' said Mary Jane, 'and finish the discussion afterwards.'

On the landing outside the drawing-room Gabriel found his wife and Mary Jane trying to persuade Miss Ivors to stay for supper. But Miss Ivors, who had put on her hat and was buttoning her cloak, would not stay. She did not feel in the least hungry and she had already overstayed her time.

'But only for ten minutes, Molly,' said Mrs Conroy. 'That won't delay you.'

'To take a pick itself,' said Mary Jane, 'after all your dancing.'

'I really couldn't,' said Miss Ivors.

'I am afraid you didn't enjoy yourself at all,' said Mary Jane hopelessly.

'Ever so much, I assure you,' said Miss Ivors, 'but you really must let me run off now.'

'But how can you get home?' asked Mrs Conroy.

'O, it's only two steps up the quay.'

Gabriel hesitated a moment and said:

'If you will allow me, Miss Ivors, I'll see you home if you are really obliged to go.'

But Miss Ivors broke away from them.

'I won't hear of it,' she cried. 'For goodness' sake go in to your suppers and don't mind me. I'm quite well able to take care of myself.'

'Well, you're the comical girl, Molly,' said Mrs Conroy frankly.

'Beannacht libh,' cried Miss Ivors, with a laugh, as she ran down the staircase.

Mary Jane gazed after her, a moody puzzled expression on her face, while Mrs Conroy leaned over the banisters to listen for the hall-door. Gabriel asked himself was he the cause of her abrupt departure. But she did not seem to be in ill humour--she had gone away laughing. He stared blankly down the staircase.

At that moment Aunt Kate came toddling out of the supper-room, almost wringing her hands in despair.

'Where is Gabriel?' she cried. 'Where on earth is Gabriel? There's everyone waiting in there, stage to let, and nobody to carve the goose!'

'Here I am, Aunt Kate!' cried Gabriel, with sudden animation, 'ready to carve a flock of geese, if necessary.'

A fat brown goose lay at one end of the table, and at the other end, on a bed of creased paper strewn with sprigs of parsley, lay a great ham, stripped of its outer skin and peppered over with crust crumbs, a neat paper frill round its shin, and beside this was a round of spiced beef. Between these rival ends ran parallel lines of side-dishes: two little minsters of jelly, red and yellow; a shallow dish full of blocks of blancmange and red jam, a large green leaf-shaped dish with a stalk-shaped handle, on which lay bunches of purple raisins and peeled almonds, a companion dish on which lay a solid rectangle of Smyrna figs, a dish of custard topped with grated nutmeg, a small bowl full of chocolates and sweets wrapped in gold and silver papers and a glass vase in which stood some tall celery stalks. In the centre of the table there stood, as sentries to a fruit-stand which upheld a pyramid of oranges and American apples, two squat old-fashioned decanters of cut glass, one containing port and the other dark sherry. On the closed square piano a pudding in a huge yellow dish lay in waiting, and behind it were three squads of bottles of stout and ale and minerals drawn up according to the colours of their uniforms, the first two black, with brown and red labels, the third and smallest squad white, with transverse green sashes.

Gabriel took his seat boldly at the head of the table and, having looked to the edge of the carver, plunged his fork firmly into the goose. He felt quite at ease now, for he was an expert carver and liked nothing better than to find himself at the head of a well-laden table.

'Miss Furlong, what shall I send you?' he asked. 'A wing

or a slice of the breast?'

'Just a small slice of the breast.'

'Miss Higgins, what for you?'

'O, anything at all, Mr Conroy.'

While Gabriel and Miss Daly exchanged plates of goose and plates of ham and spiced beef, Lily went from guest to guest with a dish of hot floury potatoes wrapped in a white napkin. This was Mary Jane's idea and she had also suggested apple sauce for the goose, but Aunt Kate had said that plain roast goose without any apple sauce had always been good enough for her and she hoped she might never eat worse. Mary Jane waited on her pupils and saw that they got the best slices, and Aunt Kate and Aunt Julia opened and carried across from the piano bottles of stout and ale for the gentlemen and bottles of minerals for the ladies. There was a great deal of confusion and laughter and noise, the noise of orders and counter-orders, of knives and forks, of corks and glass-stoppers. Gabriel began to carve second helpings as soon as he had finished the first round without serving himself. Everyone protested loudly, so that he compromised by taking a long draught of stout, for he had found the carving hot work. Mary Jane settled down quietly to her supper, but Aunt Kate and Aunt Julia were still toddling round the table, walking on each other's heels, getting in each other's way and giving each other unheeded orders. Mr Browne begged of them to sit down and eat their suppers and so did Gabriel, but they said there was time enough, so that, at last, Freddy Malins stood up and, capturing Aunt Kate, plumped her down on her chair amid general laughter.

When everyone had been well served Gabriel said, smiling:

'Now, if anyone wants a little more of what vulgar people call stuffing let him or her speak.'

A chorus of voices invited him to begin his own supper, and Lily came forward with three potatoes which she had reserved for him.

'Very well,' said Gabriel amiably, as he took another preparatory draught, 'kindly forget my existence, ladies and gentlemen, for a few minutes.'

He set to his supper and took no part in the conversation with which the table covered Lily's removal of the plates. The subject of talk was the opera company which was then at the Theatre Royal. Mr Bartell D'Arcy, the tenor, a dark-complexioned young man with a smart moustache, praised very highly the leading contralto of the company, but Miss Furlong thought she had a rather vulgar style of production. Freddy Malins said there was a Negro chieftain singing in the second part of the Gaiety pantomime who had one of the finest tenor voices he had ever heard.

'Have you heard him?' he asked Mr Bartell D'Arcy across the table.

'No,' answered Mr Bartell D'Arcy carelessly.

'Because,' Freddy Malins explained, 'now I'd be curious to hear your opinion of him. I think he has a grand voice.'

'It takes Teddy to find out the really good things,' said Mr Browne familiarly to the table.

'And why couldn't he have a voice too?' asked Freddy Malins sharply. 'Is it because he's only a black?'

Nobody answered this question and Mary Jane led the table back to the legitimate opera. One of her pupils had given her a pass for Mignon. Of course it was very fine, she said, but it made her think of poor Georgina Burns. Mr Browne could go back farther still, to the old Italian companies that used to come to Dublin--Tietjens, Ilma de

Murzka, Campanini, the great Trebelli, Giuglini, Ravelli, Aramburo. Those were the days, he said, when there was something like singing to be heard in Dublin. He told too of how the top gallery of the old Royal used to be packed night after night, of how one night an Italian tenor had sung five encores to 'Let me like a Soldier fall', introducing a high C every time, and of how the gallery boys would sometimes in their enthusiasm unyoke the horses from the carriage of some great prima donna and pull her themselves through the streets to her hotel. Why did they never play the grand old operas now, he asked, Dinorah, Lucrezia Borgia? Because they could not get the voices to sing them: that was why.

'O, well,' said Mr Bartell D'Arcy, 'I presume there are as good singers today as there were then.'

'Where are they?' asked Mr Browne defiantly.

'In London, Paris, Milan,' said Mr Bartell D'Arcy warmly. 'I suppose Caruso, for example, is quite as good, if not better than any of the men you have mentioned.'

'Maybe so,' said Mr Browne. 'But I may tell you I doubt it strongly.'

'O, I'd give anything to hear Caruso sing,' said Mary Jane.

'For me,' said Aunt Kate, who had been picking a bone, 'there was only one tenor. To please me, I mean. But I suppose none of you ever heard of him.'

'Who was he, Miss Morkan?' asked Mr Bartell D'Arcy politely.

'His name,' said Aunt Kate, 'was Parkinson. I heard him when he was in his prime and I think he had then the purest tenor voice that was ever put into a man's throat.'

'Strange,' said Mr Bartell D'Arcy. 'I never even heard of him.'

'Yes, yes, Miss Morkan is right,' said Mr Browne. 'I remember hearing old Parkinson, but he's too far back for me.'

'A beautiful, pure, sweet, mellow English tenor,' said Aunt Kate with enthusiasm.

Gabriel having finished, the huge pudding was transferred to the table. The clatter of forks and spoons began again. Gabriel's wife served out spoonfuls of the pudding and passed the plates down the table. Midway down they were held up by Mary Jane, who replenished them with raspberry or orange jelly or with blancmange and jam. The pudding was of Aunt Julia's making, and she received praises for it from all quarters. She herself said that it was not quite brown enough.

'Well, I hope, Miss Morkan,' said Mr Browne, 'that I'm brown enough for you because, you know, I'm all Brown.'

All the gentlemen, except Gabriel, ate some of the pudding out of compliment to Aunt Julia. As Gabriel never ate sweets the celery had been left for him. Freddy Malins also took a stalk of celery and ate it with his pudding. He had been told that celery was a capital thing for the blood and he was just then under doctor's care. Mrs Malins, who had been silent all through the supper, said that her son was going down to Mount Melleray in a week or so. The table then spoke of Mount Melleray, how bracing the air was down there, how hospitable the monks were and how they never asked for a penny-piece from their guests.

'And do you mean to say,' asked Mr Browne incredulously, 'that a chap can go down there and put up there as if it were a hotel and live on the fat of the land and then come away without paying anything?'

'O, most people give some donation to the monastery when they leave,' said Mary Jane.

'I wish we had an institution like that in our Church,' said Mr Browne candidly.

He was astonished to hear that the monks never spoke, got up at two in the morning and slept in their coffins. He asked what they did it for.

'That's the rule of the order,' said Aunt Kate firmly.

'Yes, but why?' asked Mr Browne.

Aunt Kate repeated that it was the rule, that was all. Mr Browne still seemed not to understand. Freddy Malins explained to him, as best he could, that the monks were trying to make up for the sins committed by all the sinners in the outside world. The explanation was not very clear, for Mr Browne grinned and said:

'I like that idea very much, but wouldn't a comfortable spring bed do them as well as a coffin?'

'The coffin,' said Mary Jane, 'is to remind them of their last end.'

As the subject had grown lugubrious it was buried in a silence of the table, during which Mrs Malins could be heard saying to her neighbour in an indistinct undertone:

'They are very good men, the monks, very pious men.'

The raisins and almonds and figs and apples and oranges and chocolates and sweets were now passed about the table, and Aunt Julia invited all the guests to have either port or sherry. At first Mr Bartell D'Arcy refused to take either, but one of his neighbours nudged him and whispered something to him, upon which he allowed his glass to be filled. Gradually as the last glasses were being filled the conversation ceased. A pause followed, broken only by the noise of the wine and by unsettling of chairs. The Misses Morkan, all three, looked down at the table-cloth. Someone coughed once or twice, and then a few gentlemen patted the table gently as a signal for silence.

The silence came and Gabriel pushed back his chair and stood up.

The patting at once grew louder in encouragement and then ceased altogether. Gabriel leaned his ten trembling fingers on the tablecloth and smiled nervously at the company. Meeting a row of upturned faces he raised his eyes to the chandelier. The piano was playing a waltz tune and he could hear the skirts sweeping against the drawing-room door. People, perhaps, were standing in the snow on the quay outside, gazing up at the lighted windows and listening to the waltz music. The air was pure there. In the distance lay the park, where the trees were weighted with snow. The Wellington Monument wore a gleaming cap of snow that flashed westwards over the white field of Fifteen Acres.

He began:

'Ladies and Gentlemen,

'It has fallen to my lot this evening, as in years past, to perform a very pleasing task, but a task for which I am afraid my poor powers as a speaker are all too inadequate.'

'No, no!' said Mr Browne.

'But, however that may be, I can only ask you tonight to take the will for the deed, and to lend me your attention for a few moments while I endeavour to express to you in words what my feelings are on this occasion.

'Ladies and Gentlemen, it is not the first time that we have gathered together under this hospitable roof, around this hospitable board. It is not the first time that we have been the recipients--or perhaps, I had better say, the victims--of the hospitality of certain good ladies.'

He made a circle in the air with his arm and paused. Everyone laughed or smiled at Aunt Kate and Aunt Julia and Mary Jane, who all turned crimson with pleasure.

Gabriel went on more boldly:

'I feel more strongly with every recurring year that our country has no tradition which does it so much honour and which it should guard so jealously as that of its hospitality. It is a tradition that is unique as far as my experience goes (and I have visited not a few places abroad) among the modern nations. Some would say, perhaps, that with us it is rather a failing than anything to be boasted of. But granted even that, it is, to my mind, a princely failing, and one that I trust will long be cultivated among us. Of one thing, at least, I am sure. As long as this one roof shelters the good ladies aforesaid--and I wish from my heart it may do so for many and many a long year to come--the tradition of genuine warm-hearted courteous Irish hospitality, which our forefathers have handed down to us and which we must hand down to our descendants, is still alive among us.'

A hearty murmur of assent ran round the table. It shot through Gabriel's mind that Miss Ivors was not there and that she had gone away discourteously: and he said with confidence in himself:

'Ladies and Gentlemen,

'A new generation is growing up in our midst, a generation actuated by new ideas and new principles. It is serious and enthusiastic for these new ideas and its enthusiasm, even when it is misdirected, is, I believe, in the main sincere. But we are living in a sceptical and, if I may use the phrase, a thought-tormented age: and sometimes I fear that this new generation, educated or hyper-educated as it is, will lack those qualities of humanity, of hospitality, of kindly humour which belonged to an older day. Listening tonight to the names of all those great singers of the past it seemed to me, I must confess, that we were living in a less spacious age. Those days might, without exaggeration, be called spacious days: and if they are gone beyond recall, let us hope, at least, that in gatherings such as this we shall still speak of them with pride and affection, still cherish in our hearts the memory of those dead and gone great ones whose fame the world will not willingly let die.'

'Hear, hear!' said Mr Browne loudly.

'But yet,' continued Gabriel, his voice falling into a softer inflection, 'there are always in gatherings such as this sadder thoughts that will recur to our minds: thoughts of the past, of youth, of changes, of absent faces that we miss here tonight. Our path through life is strewn with many such sad memories: and were we to brood upon them always we could not find the heart to go on bravely with our work among the living. We have all of us living duties and living affections which claim, and rightly claim, our strenuous endeavours.

'Therefore, I will not linger on the past. I will not let any gloomy moralizing intrude upon us here tonight. Here we are gathered together for a brief moment from the bustle and rush of our everyday routine. We are met here as friends, in the spirit of good-fellowship, as colleagues, also, to a certain extent, in the true spirit of camaraderie, and as the guests of--what shall I call them?--the Three Graces of the Dublin musical world.'

The table burst into applause and laughter at this allusion. Aunt Julia vainly asked each of her neighbours in turn to tell her what Gabriel had said.

'He says we are the Three Graces, Aunt Julia,' said Mary Jane.

Aunt Julia did not understand, but she looked up, smiling at Gabriel, who continued in the same vein:

'Ladies and Gentlemen,

'I will not attempt to play tonight the part that Paris played on another occasion. I will not attempt to choose between them. The task would be an invidious one and one beyond my poor powers. For when I view them in turn, whether it be our chief hostess herself, whose good heart, whose too good heart, has become a byword with all who know her; or her sister, who seems to be gifted with perennial youth and whose singing must have been a surprise and a revelation to us all tonight; or, last but not least, when I consider our youngest hostess, talented, cheerful, hardworking and the best of nieces, I confess, Ladies and Gentlemen, that I do not know to which of them I should award the prize.'

Gabriel glanced down at his aunts and, seeing the large smile on Aunt Julia's face and the tears which had risen to Aunt Kate's eyes, hastened to his close. He raised his glass of port gallantly, while every member of the company fingered a glass expectantly, and said loudly:

'Let us toast them all three together. Let us drink to their health, wealth, long life, happiness, and prosperity and may they long continue to hold the proud and self-won position which they hold in their profession and the position of honour and affection which they hold in our hearts.'

All the guests stood up, glass in hand, and turning towards the three seated ladies, sang in unison, with Mr Browne as leader:

For they are jolly gay fellows,
For they are jolly gay fellows,
For they are jolly gay fellows,
Which nobody can deny.

Aunt Kate was making frank use of her handkerchief and even Aunt Julia seemed moved. Freddy Malins beat

time with his pudding-fork and the singers turned towards one another, as if in melodious conference, while
they sang with emphasis:

Unless he tells a lie,
Unless he tells a lie.

Then, turning once more towards their hostesses, they
sang:

For they are jolly gay fellows,
For they are jolly gay fellows,
For they are jolly gay fellows,
Which nobody can deny.

The acclamation which followed was taken up beyond
the door of the supper-room by many of the other guests
and renewed time after time, Freddy Malins acting as officer with his fork on high.

The piercing morning air came into the hall where they
were standing so that Aunt Kate said:

'Close the door, somebody. Mrs Malins will get her
death of cold.'

'Browne is out there, Aunt Kate,' said Mary Jane.

'Browne is everywhere,' said Aunt Kate, lowering her
voice.

Mary Jane laughed at her tone.

'Really,' she said archly, 'he is very attentive.'

'He has been laid on here like the gas,' said Aunt Kate in
the same tone, 'all during the Christmas.'

She laughed herself this time good-humouredly and
then added quickly:

'But tell him to come in, Mary Jane, and close the door. I
hope to goodness he didn't hear me.'

At that moment the hall-door was opened and Mr
Browne came in from the doorstep, laughing as if his heart

would break. He was dressed in a long green overcoat with mock astrakhan cuffs and collar and wore on his head an oval fur cap. He pointed down the snow-covered quay from where the sound of shrill prolonged whistling was borne in.

'Teddy will have all the cabs in Dublin out,' he said.

Gabriel advanced from the little pantry behind the office, struggling into his overcoat and, looking round the hall, said.

'Gretta not down yet?'

'She's getting on her things, Gabriel,' said Aunt Kate.

'Who's playing up there?' asked Gabriel.

'Nobody. They're all gone.'

'O no, Aunt Kate,' said Mary Jane. 'Bartell D'Arcy and Miss O'Callaghan aren't gone yet.'

'Someone is fooling at the piano anyhow,' said Gabriel.

Mary Jane glanced at Gabriel and Mr Browne and said with a shiver:

'It makes me feel cold to look at you two gentlemen muffled up like that. I wouldn't like to face your journey home at this hour.'

'I'd like nothing better this minute,' said Mr Browne stoutly, 'than a rattling fine walk in the country or a fast drive with a good spanking goer between the shafts.'

'We used to have a very good horse and trap at home,' said Aunt Julia, sadly.

'The never-to-be-forgotten Johnny,' said Mary Jane, laughing.

Aunt Kate and Gabriel laughed too.

'Why, what was wonderful about Johnny?' asked Mr Browne.

'The late lamented Patrick Morkan, our grandfather, that is,' explained Gabriel, 'commonly known in his later years as the old gentleman, was a glue-boiler.'

'O, now, Gabriel,' said Aunt Kate, laughing, 'he had a starch mill.'

'Well, glue or starch,' said Gabriel, 'the old gentleman had a horse by the name of Johnny. And Johnny used to work in the old gentleman's mill, walking round and round in order to drive the mill. That was all very well; but now comes the tragic part about Johnny. One fine day the old gentleman thought he'd like to drive out with the quality to a military review in the park.'

'The Lord have mercy on his soul,' said Aunt Kate, compassionately.

'Amen,' said Gabriel. 'So the old gentleman, as I said, harnessed Johnny and put on his very best tall hat and his very best stock collar and drove out in grand style from his ancestral mansion somewhere near Back Lane, I think.'

Everyone laughed, even Mrs Malins, at Gabriel's manner, and Aunt Kate said:

'O, now, Gabriel, he didn't live in Back Lane, really. Only the mill was there.'

'Out from the mansion of his forefathers,' continued Gabriel, 'he drove with Johnny. And everything went on beautifully until Johnny came in sight of King Billy's statue: and whether he fell in love with the horse King Billy sits on or whether he thought he was back again in the mill, anyway he began to walk round the statue.'

Gabriel paced in a circle round the hall in his goloshes amid the laughter of the others.

'Round and round he went,' said Gabriel, 'and the old gentleman, who was a very pompous old gentleman, was highly indignant. "Go on, sir! What do you mean, sir? Johnny! Johnny! Most extraordinary conduct! Can't understand the horse!"'

The peals of laughter which followed Gabriel's imitation of the incident were interrupted by a resounding knock at the hall-door. Mary Jane ran to open it and let in Freddy Malins. Freddy Malins, with his hat well back on his head and his shoulders humped with cold, was puffing and steaming after his exertions.

'I could only get one cab,' he said.

'O, we'll find another along the quay,' said Gabriel.

'Yes,' said Aunt Kate. 'Better not keep Mrs Malins standing in the draught.'

Mrs Malins was helped down the front steps by her son and Mr Browne and, after many manoeuvres, hoisted into the cab. Freddy Malins clambered in after her and spent a long time settling her on the seat, Mr Browne helping him with advice. At last she was settled comfortably and Freddy Malins invited Mr Browne into the cab. There was a good deal of confused talk, and then Mr Browne got into the cab. The cabman settled his rug over his knees, and bent down for the address. The confusion grew greater and the cabman was directed differently by Freddy Malins and Mr Browne, each of whom had his head out through a window of the cab. The difficulty was to know where to drop Mr Browne along the route, and Aunt Kate, Aunt Julia, and Mary Jane helped the discussion from the doorstep with cross-directions and contradictions and abundance of laughter. As for Freddy Malins he was speechless with laughter. He popped his head in and out of the window every moment to the great danger of his hat, and told his mother how the discussion was progressing, till at last Mr Browne shouted to the bewildered cabman above the din of everybody's laughter:

'Do you know Trinity College?'

'Yes, sir,' said the cabman.

'Well, drive bang up against Trinity College gates,' said Mr Browne, 'and then we'll tell you where to go. You understand now?'

'Yes, sir,' said the cabman.

'Make like a bird for Trinity College.'

'Right, sir,' said the cabman.

The horse was whipped up and the cab rattled off along the quay amid a chorus of laughter and adieux.

Gabriel had not gone to the door with the others. He was in a dark part of the hall gazing up the staircase. A woman was standing near the top of the first flight, in the shadow also. He could not see her face but he could see the terra-cotta and salmon-pink panels of her skirt which the shadow made appear black and white. It was his wife. She was leaning on the banisters, listening to something. Gabriel was surprised at her stillness and strained his ear to listen also. But he could hear little save the noise of laughter and dispute on the front steps, a few chords struck on the piano and a few notes of a man's voice singing.

He stood still in the gloom of the hall, trying to catch the air that the voice was singing and gazing up at his wife. There was grace and mystery in her attitude as if she were a symbol of something. He asked himself what is a woman standing on the stairs in the shadow, listening to distant music, a symbol of. If he were a painter he would paint her in that attitude. Her blue felt hat would show off the bronze of her hair against the darkness and the dark panels of her skirt would show off the light ones. Distant Music he would call the picture if he were a painter.

The hall-door was closed, and Aunt Kate, Aunt Julia, and Mary Jane came down the hall, still laughing.

'Well, isn't Freddy terrible?' said Mary Jane. 'He's really

terrible.'

Gabriel said nothing, but pointed up the stairs towards where his wife was standing. Now that the hall-door was closed the voice and the piano could be heard more clearly. Gabriel held up his hand for them to be silent. The song seemed to be in the old Irish tonality and the singer seemed uncertain both of his words and of his voice. The voice, made plaintive by distance and by the singer's hoarseness, faintly illuminated the cadence of the air with words expressing grief:

O, the rain falls on my heavy locks
And the dew wets my skin,
My babe lies cold...

'O,' exclaimed Mary Jane. 'It's Bartell D'Arcy singing, and he wouldn't sing all the night. O, I'll get him to sing a song before he goes.'

'O, do, Mary Jane,' said Aunt Kate.

Mary Jane brushed past the others and ran to the staircase, but before she reached it the singing stopped and the piano was closed abruptly.

'O, what a pity!' she cried. 'Is he coming down, Gretta?'

Gabriel heard his wife answer yes and saw her come down towards them. A few steps behind her were Mr Bartell D'Arcy and Miss O'Callaghan.

'O, Mr D'Arcy,' cried Mary Jane, 'it's downright mean of you to break off like that when we were all in raptures listening to you.'

'I have been at him all the evening,' said Miss O'Callaghan, 'and Mrs Conroy, too, and he told us he had a dreadful cold and couldn't sing.'

'O, Mr D'Arcy,' said Aunt Kate, 'now that was a great fib to tell.'

'Can't you see that I'm as hoarse as a crow?' said Mr

D'Arcy roughly.

He went into the pantry hastily and put on his overcoat. The others, taken back by his rude speech, could find nothing to say. Aunt Kate wrinkled her brows and made signs to the others to drop the subject. Mr D'Arcy stood swathing his neck carefully and frowning.

'It's the weather,' said Aunt Julia, after a pause.

'Yes, everybody has colds,' said Aunt Kate readily, 'everybody.'

'They say,' said Mary Jane, 'we haven't had snow like it for thirty years, and I read this morning in the newspapers that the snow is general all over Ireland.'

'I love the look of snow,' said Aunt Julia sadly.

'So do I,' said Miss O'Callaghan. 'I think Christmas is never really Christmas unless we have the snow on the ground.'

'But poor Mr D'Arcy doesn't like the snow,' said Aunt Kate, smiling.

Mr D'Arcy came from the pantry, fully swathed and buttoned, and in a repentant tone told them the history of his cold. Everyone gave him advice and said it was a great pity and urged him to be very careful of his throat in the night air. Gabriel watched his wife, who did not join in the conversation. She was standing right under the dusty fanlight and the flame of the gas lit up the rich bronze of her hair, which he had seen her drying at the fire a few days before. She was in the same attitude and seemed un-aware of the talk about her. At last she turned towards them and Gabriel saw that there was colour on her cheeks and that her eyes were shining. A sudden tide of joy went leaping out of his heart.

'Mr D'Arcy,' she said, 'what is the name of that song you were singing?'

'It's called "The Lass of Aughrim",' said Mr D'Arcy, 'but I couldn't remember it properly. Why? Do you know it?'

'"The Lass of Aughrim",' she repeated. 'I couldn't think of the name.'

'It's a very nice air,' said Mary Jane. 'I'm sorry you were not in voice tonight.'

'Now, Mary Jane,' said Aunt Kate, 'don't annoy Mr D'Arcy. I won't have him annoyed.'

Seeing that all were ready to start she shepherded them to the door, where good night was said:

'Well, good night, Aunt Kate, and thanks for the pleasant evening.'

'Good night, Gabriel. Good night, Gretta!'

'Good night, Aunt Kate, and thanks ever so much. Good night, Aunt Julia.'

'O, good night, Gretta, I didn't see you.'

'Good night, Mr D'Arcy. Good night, Miss O'Callaghan.'

'Good night, Miss Morkan.'

'Good night, again.'

'Good night, all. Safe home.'

'Good night. Good night.'

The morning was still dark. A dull, yellow light brooded over the houses and the river; and the sky seemed to be descending. It was slushy underfoot, and only streaks and patches of snow lay on the roofs, on the parapets of the quay and on the area railings. The lamps were still burning redly in the murky air and, across the river, the palace of the Four Courts stood out menacingly against the heavy sky.

She was walking on before him with Mr Bartell D'Arcy, her shoes in a brown parcel tucked under one arm and her hands holding her skirt up from the slush. She had no longer any grace of attitude, but Gabriel's eyes were still bright with happiness. The blood went bounding along his veins and the thoughts went rioting through his brain, proud, joyful, tender, valorous.

She was walking on before him so lightly and so erect that he longed to run after her noiselessly, catch her by the shoulders and say something foolish and affectionate into her ear. She seemed to him so frail that he longed to defend her against something and then to be alone with her. Moments of their secret life together burst like stars upon his memory. A heliotrope envelope was lying beside his breakfast-cup and he was caressing it with his hand. Birds were twittering in the ivy and the sunny web of the curtain was shimmering along the floor: he could not eat for happiness. They were standing on the crowded platform and he was placing a ticket inside the warm palm of her glove. He was standing with her in the cold, looking in through a grated window at a man making bottles in a roaring furnace. It was very cold. Her face, fragrant in the cold air, was quite close to his, and suddenly he called out to the man at the furnace:

'Is the fire hot, sir?'

But the man could not hear with the noise of the furnace. It was just as well. He might have answered rudely.

A wave of yet more tender joy escaped from his heart and went coursing in warm flood along his arteries. Like the tender fire of stars moments of their life together, that no one knew of or would ever know of, broke upon and illumined his memory. He longed to recall to her those moments, to make her forget the years of their dull existence together and remember only their moments of ecstasy. For the years, he felt, had not quenched his soul or hers. Their children, his writing, her household cares had not quenched all their souls' tender fire. In one letter that he had written to her then he had said: 'Why is it that words like these seem to me so dull and cold? Is it because there is no word tender enough to be your name?'

Like distant music these words that he had written years before were borne towards him from the past. He longed to be alone with her. When the others had gone away, when he and she were in the room in their hotel, then they would be alone together. He would call her softly:

'Gretta!'

Perhaps she would not hear at once: she would be undressing. Then something in his voice would strike her. She would turn and look at him...

At the corner of Winetavern Street they met a cab. He was glad of its rattling noise as it saved him from conversation. She was looking out of the window and seemed tired. The others spoke only a few words, pointing out some building or street. The horse galloped along wearily under the murky morning sky, dragging his old rattling box after his heels, and Gabriel was again in a cab with her, galloping to catch the boat, galloping to their honeymoon.

As the cab drove across O'Connell Bridge Miss O'Callaghan said:

'They say you never cross O'Connell Bridge without seeing a white horse.'

'I see a white man this time,' said Gabriel.

'Where?' asked Mr Bartell D'Arcy.

Gabriel pointed to the statue, on which lay patches of snow. Then he nodded familiarly to it and waved his hand.

'Good night, Dan,' he said gaily.

When the cab drew up before the hotel, Gabriel jumped

out and, in spite of Mr Bartell D'Arcy's protest, paid the driver. He gave the man a shilling over his fare. The man saluted and said:

'A prosperous New Year to you, sir.'

'The same to you,' said Gabriel cordially.

She leaned for a moment on his arm in getting out of the cab and while standing at the kerb-stone, bidding the others good night. She leaned lightly on his arm, as lightly as when she had danced with him a few hours before. He had felt proud and happy then, happy that she was his, proud of her grace and wifely carriage. But now, after the kindling again of so many memories, the first touch of her body, musical and strange and perfumed, sent through him a keen pang of lust. Under cover of her silence he pressed her arm closely to his side, and, as they stood at the hotel door, he felt that they had escaped from their lives and duties, escaped from home and friends and run away together with wild and radiant hearts to a new adventure.

An old man was dozing in a great hooded chair in the hall. He lit a candle in the office and went before them to the stairs. They followed him in silence, their feet falling in soft thuds on the thickly carpeted stairs. She mounted the stairs behind the porter, her head bowed in the ascent, her frail shoulders curved as with a burden, her skirt girt tightly about her. He could have flung his arms about her hips and held her still, for his arms were trembling with desire to seize her and only the stress of his nails against the palms of his hands held the wild impulse of his body in check. The porter halted on the stairs to settle his guttering candle. They halted, too, on the steps below him. In the silence Gabriel could hear the falling of molten wax into the tray and the thumping of his own heart against his ribs.

The porter led them along a corridor and opened a door. Then he set his unstable candle down on a toilet-table and asked at what hour they were to be called in the morning.

'Eight,' said Gabriel.

The porter pointed to the tap of the electric-light and began a muttered apology, but Gabriel cut him short.

'We don't want any light. We have light enough from the street. And I say,' he added, pointing to the candle, 'you might remove that handsome article, like a good man.'

The porter took up his candle again, but slowly, for he was surprised by such a novel idea. Then he mumbled good night and went out. Gabriel shot the lock to.

A ghastly light from the street lamp lay in a long shaft from one window to the door. Gabriel threw his overcoat and hat on a couch and crossed the room towards the window. He looked down into the street in order that his emotion might calm a little. Then he turned and leaned against a chest of drawers with his back to the light. She had taken off her hat and cloak and was standing before a large swinging mirror, unhooking her waist. Gabriel paused for a few moments, watching her, and then said:

'Gretta!'

She turned away from the mirror slowly and walked along the shaft of light towards him. Her face looked so serious and weary that the words would not pass Gabriel's lips. No, it was not the moment yet.

'You looked tired,' he said.

'I am a little,' she answered.

'You don't feel ill or weak?'

'No, tired: that's all.'

She went on to the window and stood there, looking out. Gabriel waited again and then, fearing that diffidence was about to conquer him, he said abruptly:

'By the way, Gretta!'

'What is it?'

'You know that poor fellow Malins?' he said quickly.

'Yes. What about him?'

'Well, poor fellow, be's a decent sort of chap, after all,' continued Gabriel in a false voice. 'He gave me back that sovereign I lent him, and I didn't expect it, really. It's a pity he wouldn't keep away from that Browne, because he's not a bad fellow, really.'

He was trembling now with annoyance. Why did she seem so abstracted? He did not know how he could begin. Was she annoyed, too, about something? If she would only turn to him or come to him of her own accord! To take her as she was would be brutal. No, he must see some ardour in her eyes first. He longed to be master of her strange mood.

'When did you lend him the pound?' she asked, after a pause.

Gabriel strove to restrain himself from breaking out into brutal language about the sottish Malins and his pound. He longed to cry to her from his soul, to crush her body against his, to overmaster her. But he said:

'O, at Christmas, when he opened that little Christmas-card shop, in Henry Street.'

He was in such a fever of rage and desire that he did not hear her come from the window. She stood before him for an instant, looking at him strangely. Then, suddenly raising herself on tiptoe and resting her hands lightly on his shoulders, she kissed him.

'You are a very generous person, Gabriel,' she said.

Gabriel, trembling with delight at her sudden kiss and at the quaintness of her phrase, put his hands on her hair and began smoothing it back, scarcely touching it with his fingers. The washing had made it fine and brilliant. His heart was brimming over with happiness. Just when he was wishing for it she had come to him of her own accord. Perhaps her thoughts had been running with his. Perhaps she had felt the impetuous desire that was in him, and then the yielding mood had come upon her. Now that she had fallen to him so easily, he wondered why he had been so diffident.

He stood, holding her head between his hands. Then, slipping one arm swiftly about her body and drawing her towards him, he said softly:

'Gretta, dear, what are you thinking about?'

She did not answer nor yield wholly to his arm. He said again, softly:

'Tell me what it is, Gretta. I think I know what is the matter. Do I know?'

She did not answer at once. Then she said in an outburst of tears:

'O, I am thinking about that song, "The Lass of Aughrim".'

She broke loose from him and ran to the bed and, throwing her arms across the bed-rail, hid her face. Gabriel stood stock-still for a moment in astonishment and then followed her. As he passed in the way of the cheval-glass he caught sight of himself in full length, his broad, well-filled shirt-front, the face whose expression always puzzled him when he saw it in a mirror, and his glimmering gilt-rimmed eye-glasses. He halted a few paces from her and said:

'What about the song? Why does that make you cry?'

She raised her head from her arms and dried her eyes with the back of her hand like a child. A kinder note than he had intended went into his voice.

'Why, Gretta?' he asked.

'I am thinking about a person long ago who used to sing that song.'

'And who was the person long ago?' asked Gabriel, smiling.

'It was a person I used to know in Galway when I was living with my grandmother,' she said.

The smile passed away from Gabriel's face. A dull anger began to gather again at the back of his mind and the dull fires of his lust began to glow angrily in his veins.

'Someone you were in love with?' he asked ironically.

'It was a young boy I used to know,' she answered, 'named Michael Furey. He used to sing that song, "The Lass of Aughrim". He was very delicate.'

Gabriel was silent. He did not wish her to think that he was interested in this delicate boy.

'I can see him so plainly,' she said, after a moment. 'Such eyes as he had: big, dark eyes! And such an expression in them--an expression!'

'O, then, you were in love with him?' said Gabriel.

'I used to go out walking with him,' she said, 'when I was in Galway.'

A thought flew across Gabriel's mind.

'Perhaps that was why you wanted to go to Galway with that Ivors girl?' he said coldly.

She looked at him and asked in surprise:

'What for?'

Her eyes made Gabriel feel awkward. He shrugged his shoulders and said:

'How do I know? To see him, perhaps.'

She looked away from him along the shaft of light towards the window in silence.

'He is dead,' she said at length. 'He died when he was only seventeen. Isn't it a terrible thing to die so young as that?'

'What was he?' asked Gabriel, still ironically.

'He was in the gasworks,' she said.

Gabriel felt humiliated by the failure of his irony and by the evocation of this figure from the dead, a boy in the gasworks. While he had been full of memories of their secret life together, full of tenderness and joy and desire, she had been comparing him in her mind with another. A shameful consciousness of his own person assailed him. He saw himself as a ludicrous figure, acting as a pennyboy for his aunts, a nervous, well-meaning sentimentalist, orating to vulgarians and idealizing his own clownish lusts, the pitiable fatuous fellow he had caught a glimpse of in the mirror. Instinctively he turned his back more to the light lest she might see the shame that burned upon his forehead.

He tried to keep up his tone of cold interrogation, but his voice when he spoke was humble and indifferent.

'I suppose you were in love with this Michael Furey, Gretta,' he said.

'I was great with him at that time,' she said.

Her voice was veiled and sad. Gabriel, feeling now how vain it would be to try to lead her whither he had purposed, caressed one of her hands and said, also sadly:

'And what did he die of so young, Gretta? Consumption, was it?'

'I think he died for me,' she answered.

A vague terror seized Gabriel at this answer, as if, at that hour when he had hoped to triumph, some impalpable and vindictive being was coming against him, gathering forces against him in its vague world. But he shook himself free of it with an effort of reason and continued to caress her hand. He did not question her again, for he felt that she would tell him of herself. Her hand was warm and moist: it did not respond to his touch, but he continued to caress it just as he had caressed her first letter to him that spring morning.

'It was in the winter,' she said, 'about the beginning of the winter when I was going to leave my grandmother's and come up here to the convent. And he was ill at the time in his lodgings in Galway and wouldn't be let out, and his people in Oughterard were written to. He was in decline, they said, or something like that. I never knew rightly.'

She paused for a moment and sighed.

'Poor fellow,' she said. 'He was very fond of me and he was such a gentle boy. We used to go out together, walking, you know, Gabriel, like the way they do in the country. He was going to study singing only for his health. He had a very good voice, poor Michael Furey.'

'Well; and then?' asked Gabriel.

'And then when it came to the time for me to leave Galway and come up to the convent he was much worse and I wouldn't be let see him, so I wrote him a letter saying I was going up to Dublin and would be back in the summer, and hoping he would be better then.'

She paused for a moment to get her voice under control, and then went on:

'Then the night before I left, I was in my grandmother's house in Nuns' Island, packing up, and I heard gravel thrown up against the window. The window was so wet I couldn't see, so I ran downstairs as I was and slipped out the back into the garden and there was the poor fellow at the end of the garden, shivering.'

'And did you not tell him to go back?' asked Gabriel.

'I implored of him to go home at once and told him he would get his death in the rain. But he said he did not want to live. I can see his eyes as well as well! He was standing at the end of the wall where there was a tree.'

'And did he go home?' asked Gabriel.

'Yes, he went home. And when I was only a week in the convent he died and he was buried in Oughterard, where his people came from. O, the day I heard that, that he was dead!'

She stopped, choking with sobs, and, overcome by emotion, flung herself face downward on the bed, sobbing in the quilt. Gabriel held her hand for a moment longer, irresolutely, and then, shy of intruding on her grief, let it fall gently and walked quietly to the window.

She was fast asleep.

Gabriel, leaning on his elbow, looked for a few moments unresentfully on her tangled hair and half-open mouth, listening to her deep-drawn breath. So she had had that romance in her life: a man had died for her sake. It hardly pained him now to think how poor a part he, her husband, had played in her life. He watched her while she slept, as though he and she had never lived together as man and wife. His curious eyes rested long upon her face and on her hair: and, as he thought of what she must have been then, in that time of her first girlish beauty, a strange, friendly pity for her entered his soul. He did not like to say even to himself that her face was no longer beautiful, but he knew that it was no longer the face for which Michael Furey had braved death.

118

Perhaps she had not told him all the story. His eyes moved to the chair over which she had thrown some of her clothes. A petticoat string dangled to the floor. One boot stood upright, its limp upper fallen down: the fellow of it lay upon its side. He wondered at his riot of emotions of an hour before. From what had it proceeded? From his aunt's supper, from his own foolish speech, from the wine and dancing, the merry-making when saying good night in the hall, the pleasure of the walk along the river in the snow. Poor Aunt Julia! She, too, would soon be a shade with the shade of Patrick Morkan and his horse. He had caught that haggard look upon her face for a moment when she was singing 'Arrayed for the Bridal'. Soon, per-haps, he would be sitting in that same drawing-room, dressed in black, his silk hat on his knees. The blinds would be drawn down and Aunt Kate would be sitting beside him, crying and blowing her nose and telling him how Julia had died. He would cast about in his mind for some words that might console her, and would find only lame and useless ones. Yes, yes: that would happen very soon.

The air of the room chilled his shoulders. He stretched himself cautiously along under the sheets and lay down beside his wife. One by one, they were all becoming shades. Better pass boldly into that other world, in the full glory of some passion, than fade and wither dismally with age. He thought of how she who lay beside him had locked in her heart for so many years that image of her lover's eyes when he had told her that he did not wish to live.

Generous tears filled Gabriel's eyes. He had never felt like that himself towards any woman, but he knew that such a feeling must be love. The tears gathered more thickly in his eyes and in the partial darkness he imagined he saw the form of a young man standing under a dripping tree. Other forms were near. His soul had approached that region where dwell the vast hosts of the dead. He was conscious of, but could not apprehend, their wayward and flickering existence. His own identity was fading out into a grey impalpable world: the solid world itself, which these dead had one time reared and lived in, was dissolving and dwindling.

A few light taps upon the pane made him turn to the window. It had begun to snow again. He watched sleepily the flakes, silver and dark, falling obliquely against the lamplight. The time had come for him to set out on his journey westward. Yes, the newspapers were right: snow was general all over Ireland. It was falling on every part of the dark central plain, on the treeless hills, falling softly upon the Bog of Allen and, farther westward, softly falling into the dark mutinous Shannon waves. It was falling, too, upon every part of the lonely churchyard on the hill where Michael Furey lay buried. It lay thickly drifted on the crooked crosses and headstones, on the spears of the little gate, on the barren thorns. His soul swooned slowly as he heard the snow falling faintly through the universe and faintly falling, like the descent of their last end, upon all the living and the dead.[4]

---

[4] from the short story collection Dubliners, 1914

VIII   The Inn
By Guy de Maupassant

LIKE all the little wooden inns in the higher Alps, tiny auberges situated in the bare and rocky gorges which intersect the white summits of the mountains, the inn of Schwarenbach is a refuge for travelers who are crossing the Gemmi.

It is open six months in the year and is inhabited by the family of Jean Hauser. As soon as the snow begins to fall and fills the valley so as to the road down to Loëche impassable, the father, with mother, daughter and the three sons, depart, leaving the house in charge of the old guide, Gaspard Hari, with the young guide, Ulrich Kunsi, and Sam, the great mountain dog.

The two men and the dog remain till spring in their snowy prison, with nothing before their eyes except immense, white slopes of the Balmhorn. surrounded by light, glistening summits and shut up, blocked up and buried by the snow which rises around them, enveloping and almost burying the little house up to the eaves.

It was the day on which the Hauser family were going to return to Loëche, winter was approaching and the descent was becoming dangerous. Three mules started first, laden with baggage and led by the three sons. Then the mother, Jeanne Hauser, and her daughter Louise mounted a fourth mule and set off in their turn. The father followed them, accompanied by the two men in charge, First of all who were to escort the family as far as the brow of the descent. They skirted the small lake, now frozen over, at the foot of the mass of rocks which stretched in front of the inn; then they followed the valley which was dominated on all sides by snow-covered peaks.

A ray of sunlight glinted into that little white, glistening, frozen desert, illuminating it with a cold and dazzling flame. No living thing appeared among this ocean of hills; there was no stir in that immeasurable solitude, no noise disturbed the profound silence.

By degrees the young guide, Ulrich Kunsi, a tall, long-legged Swiss, left Daddy Hauser and old Gaspard behind in order to catch up with the mule which carried the two women. The younger one looked at him as he approached, as if she would call him with her sad eyes. She was a young,. light-haired peasant girl, whose milk-white cheeks and pale hair seemed to have lost their color by long dwelling amid the ice. When Ulrich had caught up with the animal which carried the women he put his hand on the crupper and relaxed his speed. Mother Hauser began to talk to him and enumerated with minutest detail all that he would have to attend to during the winter. It was the first winter he would spend up there, while old Hari had already spent fourteen winters amid the snow at the inn of Schwarenbach.

Ulrich Kunsi listened without appearing to understand and looked incessantly at the girl. From time to time he replied: "Yes, Madame Hauser," but his thoughts seemed far away, and his calm features remained unmoved. They reached Lake Daube, whose broad, frozen surface reached to the bottom of the valley. On the right the Daubenhorn showed its black mass, rising up in a peak above the enormous moraines of the Lömmeon glacier which soared above the Wildstrubel. As they approached the neck of the Gemmi, where the descent to Loëche begins, the immense horizon of the Alps of the Valais, from which the broad, deep valley of the Rhône separated them, came in view.

In the distance there was a group of white, unequal, flat

or pointed mountain summits which glistened in the sun: the Mischabel with its twin peaks, the huge group of the Weisshorn, the heavy Brunegghorn, the lofty and formidable pyramid of Mont Cervin, slayer of men, and the Dent Blanche, that terrible coquette.

Then beneath them, as at the bottom of a terrible abyss, they saw Loëche, its houses looking like grains of sand which had been thrown into that enormous crevice which finishes and closes the Gemmi and which opens down below on to the Rhône.

The mule stopped at the edge of the path which turns and twists fantastically and the steep side of the mountain as far as the almost invisible little village at its feet. The women jumped into the snow, and the two old men joined them.

"Well," Father Hauser said, "good-by and keep up your spirits till next year, my friends," and old Hari replied: "Till next year.

They embraced each other, and then Mme Hauser in her turn offered her cheek, and the girl did the same. When Ulrich Kunsi's turn came he whispered in Louise's ear:

"Do not forget those up yonder," and she replied: "No," in such a low voice that he guessed what she had said without hearing it.

"Well, adieu," Jean Hauser repeated, "and don't fall in." Then, going before the two women, he commenced the descent, and soon all three disappeared at the first turn in the road, while the two men returned to the inn at Schwarenbach.

They walked slowly side by side without speaking. The parting was over, and they would be alone together for four or five months. Then Gaspard Hari began to relate his life last winter. He had remained with Michael Canol, who was too old now to stand it, for an accident might happen during that long solitude. They had not been dull, however, the only thing was to be resigned to it from the first, and in the end one would find plenty of distraction, games and other means of whiling away the time.

Ulrich Kunsi listened to him with his eyes on the ground, for in thought he was with those who were descending to the village. They soon came in sight of the inn which was scarcely visible, so small did it look, a mere black speck at the foot of that enormous billow of snow. When they opened the door Sam, the great curly dog, began to romp round them.

"Come, my boy," old, Gaspard said, "we have no women now, so we must get our own dinner ready. Go and peel the potatoes." And they both sat down on wooden stools and began to put the bread into the soup.

The next morning seemed very long to Kunsi. Old Hari smoked and smoked beside the hearth, while the young man looked out of the window at the snow-covered mountain opposite the house. In the afternoon he went out and, going over the previous day's ground again, he looked for the traces of the mule that had carried the two women; then when he had reached the neck of the Gemmi he laid himself down on his stomach and looked at Loëche.

The village, in its rocky pit, was not yet buried under the snow, although the white masses came quite close to it, balked, however, of their prey by the pine woods which protected the hamlet. From his vantage point the low houses looked like paving stones in a large meadow. Hauser's little daughter was there now in one of those gray-colored houses. In which? Ulrich Kunsi was too far away to be able to make them out separately. How he would have liked to go down while he was yet able!

But the sun had disappeared behind the lofty crest of the Wildstrubel, and the young man returned to the chalet. Daddy Hari was smoking and, when he saw his mate come in, proposed a game of cards to him. They sat down opposite each other for a long time and played the simple game called brisque; then they had supper and went to bed.

The following days were like the first, bright and cold, without any more snow. Old Gaspard spent his afternoons in watching the eagles and other rare birds which ventured on to those frozen heights, while Ulrich journeyed regularly to the neck of the Gemmi to look at the village. In the evening they played at cards, dice or dominoes and lost and won trifling sums, just to create an interest in the game.

One morning Hari, who was up first, called his companion. A moving cloud of white spray, deep and light, was falling on them noiselessly and burying them by degrees under a dark, thick coverlet of foam. This lasted four days and four nights. It was necessary to free the door and the windows, to dig out a passage and to cut steps to get over this frozen powder which a twelve-hour frost had made as hard as the granite of the moraines.

They lived like prisoners, not venturing outside their abode. They had divided their duties and performed them regularly. Ulrich Kunsi undertook the scouring, washing, and everything that belonged to cleanliness. He also chopped up the wood, while Gaspard Hari did the cooking and attended to the fire. Their regular and monotonous work was relieved by long games at cards or dice, but they never quarreled and were always calm and placid. They were never even impatient or ill humored,

125

nor did they ever use hand words, for they had laid in a stock of patience for this wintering on the top of the mountain.

Sometimes old Gaspard took his rifle and went after chamois and occasionally killed one. Then there was a feast in the inn at Schwarenbach, and they reveled in fresh meat. One morning ,he went our as usual. The thermometer outside marked eighteen degrees of frost, and as the sun had not yet risen, the hunter hoped to surprise the animals at the approaches to the Wildstrubel. Ulrich, being alone, remained in bed until ten o'clock. He was of a sleepy nature but would not have dared to give way like that to his inclination in the presence of the old guide, who was ever an early riser. He breakfasted leisurely with Sam, who also spent his days and nights in sleeping in front of the fire; then he felt low-spirited and even frightened at the solitude and was seized by a longing for his daily game of cards, as one is by the domination of an invincible habit. So he went out to meet his companion who was to return at four o'clock.

The snow had leveled the whole deep valley, filled up the crevasses, obliterated all signs of the two lakes and covered the rocks, so that between the high summits there was nothing but an immense white, regular, dazzling and frozen surface. For three weeks Ulnich had not been to the edge of the precipice from which he had looked down onto the village, and he wanted to go there before climbing the slopes which led to the Wildstrubel. Loëche was now covered by the snow, and the houses could scarcely be distinguished, hidden as they were by that white cloak.

Turning to the right, Ulrich reached the Lömmeon glacier. He strode along with a mountaineer's long swinging pace, striking the snow, which was as hard as a rock, with his iron-shod stick and with piercing eyes looking for the little black, moving speck in the distance on that enormous white expanse.

When he reached the end of the glacier he stopped, and asked himself whether the old man had taken that road, and then he began to walk along the moraines with rapid and uneasy steps. The day was declining; the snow was assuming a rosy tint, and a dry, frozen wind blew in rough gusts over its crystal surface. Ulrich uttered a long, shrill, vibrating call. His voice sped through the deathlike silence in which the mountains were sleeping; it reached into the distance over the profound and motionless waves of glacial foam, like the cry of a bird over the waves of the sea; then it died away, and nothing answered him.

He started off again. The sun had sunk behind the mountaintops which still were purpled with the reflection from the heavens, but the depths of the valley were becoming gray, and suddenly the young man felt frightened. It seemed to him as if the silence, the cold, the solitude, the wintry death of these mountains, were taking possession of him, were stopping and freezing his blood, making his limbs grow stiff and turning him into a motionless and frozen object, and he began to run rapidly toward the dwelling. The old man, he thought, would have returned during his absence. He had probably taken another road and would, no doubt, be sitting before the fire with a dead chamois at his feet.

He soon came in sight of the inn, but no smoke rose from it. Ulrich ran faster. Opening the door, he met Sam who ran up to him to greet him, but Gaspard Hari had not returned. Kunsi, in his alarm, turned round suddenly, as if he had expected to find his comrade hidden in a corner. Then he re-lighted the fire and made the soup, hoping every moment to see the old man come in. From time to time he went out to see if Gaspard were not in sight, It was night now, that wan night of the mountain, a livid night with the crescent moon, yellow and dim, just disappearing behind the mountaintops and shining faintly on the edge of the horizon. Then the young man went in and sat down to warm his hands and feet, while he pictured to himself every possible sort of accident. Gaspard might have broken a leg, have fallen into a crevasse, have taken a false step and dislocated his ankle. Perhaps he was lying on the snow, overcome and stiff with the cold, in agony of mind, lost and perhaps shouting for help, calling with all his might in the silence of the night.

But where? The mountain was so vast, so rugged, so dangerous in places, especially at that time of the year, that it would have required ten or twenty guides walking for a week in all directions to find a man in that immense space. Ulrich Kunsi, however, made up his mind to set out with Sam if Gaspard did not return by one in the morning, and he made his preparations. He put provisions for two days into a bag, took his steel climbing irons, tied a long, thin, strong rope round his waist and looked to see that his iron-shod stick and his ax, which served to cut steps in the ice, were in order. Then he waited. The fire was burning on the hearth; the great dog was snoring in front of it, and the clock was ticking in its case of resounding wood, as regularly as a heart beating.

He waited, his ears on the alert for distant sounds, and shivered when the wind blew against the roof and the walls. It struck twelve, and he trembled. Then, as he felt frightened and shivery, he put some water on the fire so that he might have hot coffee before starting. When the clock struck one he got up, woke Sam, opened the door and went off in the direction of the Wildstrubel. For five hours he ascended, scaling the rocks by means of his climbing irons, cutting into the ice, advancing continually and occasionally hauling up the dog, who remained below at the foot of some slope that was too steep for him, by means of the rope. About six o'clock he reached one of the summits to which old Gaspard often came after chamois, and he waited till it should be daylight.

The sky was growing pale overhead, and suddenly a strange light, springing, nobody could tell whence, suddenly illuminated the immense ocean of pale mountain peaks which stretched for many leagues around him. It seemed as if this vague brightness arose from the snow itself in order to spread itself into space. By degrees the highest and most distant summits assumed a delicate, fleshlike rose color and the red sun appeared behind the ponderous giants of the Bernese Alps.

Ulrich Kunsi set off again, walking like a hunter, stooping and looking for any traces and saying to his dog: "Seek old fellow, seek!"

He was descending the mountain now, scanning the depths closely and from time to time shouting, uttering a loud, prolonged, familiar cry which soon died away in that silent vastness, Then he put his ear to the ground to listen.

He thought he could distinguishh a voice, and so he began to run and shout again. But he heard nothing more and sat down, worn out and in despair. Toward midday he breakfasted and gave Sam, who was as tired as himself, something to eat also; then he recommenced his search.

When evening came he was still walking, having traveled more than thirty miles over the mountains. As he was too far away to return home and too tired to drag himself along any farther, he dug a hole in the snow and crouched in it with his dog under a blanket which he had brought with him. The man and the dog lay side by side, warming themselves one against the ether, but frozen to the marrow nevertheless. Ulrich scarcely slept, his mind haunted by visions and his limbs shaking with cold. Day was breaking when he got up. His legs were as stiff as iron bars, and his spirits so low that he was ready to weep, while his heart was beating so that he almost fell with excitement whenever he thought he heard a noise.

Suddenly he imagined that he also was going to die of cold in the midst of this vast solitude. The terror of such a death roused his energies and gave him renewed vigor. He was descending toward the inn, falling down and getting up again, and followed at a distance by Sam, who was limping on three legs. They did not reach Schwarenbach until four o'clock in the afternoon. The house was empty, and the young man made a fire, had something to eat and went to sleep, so worn out that he did not think of anything more.

He slept for a long time, for a very long time, the unconquerable sleep of exhaustion. But suddenly a voice, a cry, a name: "Ulrich," aroused him from his profound slumber and made him sit up in bed. Had he been dreaming? Was it one of those strange appeals which cross the dreams of disquieted minds? No, he heard it still, that reverberating cry which had entered at his ears and remained in his brain, thrilling him to the tips of his sinewy fingers. Certainly somebody had cried out and called: "Ulrich!" There was somebody there near the house, there could be no doubt of that, and he opened the door and shouted: "Is it you, Gaspard?" with all the strength of his lungs. But there was no reply, no murmur, no groan, nothing. It was quite dark, and the snow looked wan.

The wind had risen, that icy wind which cracks the rocks and leaves nothing alive on those deserted heights. It came in sudden gusts, more parching and more deadly than the burning wind of the desert, and again Ulrich shouted: "Gaspard!. Gaspard! Gaspard!" Then he waited again. Everything was silent on the mountain! Then he shook with terror, and with a bound he was inside the inn. He shut and bolted the door and then fell into a chair, trembling all over, for he felt certain that his comrade had called him at the moment of dissolution.

He was certain of that, as certain as one is of conscious life or of taste when eating. Old Gaspard Hari had been dying for two days and three nights somewhere, in some hole in one of those deep, untrodden ravines whose whiteness is more sinister than subterranean darkness. He had been dying for two days and three nights and he had just then died, thinking of his comrade. His soul, almost before it was released, had taken its flight to the inn where Ulrich was sleeping, and it had called him by that terrible and mysterious power which the spirits of the dead possess. That voiceless soul had cried to the worn-out soul of the sleeper; it had uttered its last farewell, or its reproach, or its curse on the man who had not searched carefully enough.

And Ulrich felt that it was there, quite close to him, behind the wall, behind the door which he had just fastened. It was wandering about like a night bird which skims a lighted window with his wings, and the terrified young man was ready to scream with horror. He wanted to run away but did not dare go out; he did nor dare and would never dare in the future, for the phantom would remain there day and night round the inn, as long as the old man's

131

body was not recovered and deposited in the consecrated earth of a churchyard.

Daylight came, and Kunsi recovered some of his courage with the return of the bright sun. He prepared his meal, gave his dog some food and then remained motionless on a chair, tortured at heart as he thought of the old man lying on the snow. Then as soon as night once more covered the mountains, new terrors assailed him. He now walked up and down the dark kitchen which was scarcely lighted by the flame of one candle. He walked from one end of it to the other with great strides, listening, listening to hear the terrible cry of the preceding night again break the dreary silence outside. He felt himself alone, unhappy man, as no man had ever been alone before! Alone in this immense desert of snow, alone five thousand feet above the inhabited earth, above human habitations, above that stirring, noisy, palpitating life, alone under an icy sky! A mad longing impelled him to run away, no matter where, to get down to Loëche by flinging himself over the precipice, but he did not even dare to open the door, as he felt sure that the other, the dead, man would bar his road, so that he might not be obliged to remain up there alone.

Toward midnight, tired with walking, worn out by grief and fear, he fell into a doze in his chair, for he was afraid of his bed, as one is of a haunted spot. But suddenly the strident cry of the preceding evening pierced his ears, so shrill that Ulrich stretched out his arms to repulse the ghost, and he fell onto his back with his chair.

Sam, who was awakened by the noise, began to howl as frightened dogs do and trotted all about the house, trying to find out where the danger came from. When he got to the door he sniffed beneath it, smelling vigorously, with

132

his coat bristling and his tail stiff while he growled angrily. Kunsi, who was terrified, jumped up and, holding his chair by one leg, cried "Don't come in; don't come in, or I shall kill you." And the dog, excited by this threat, barked angrily at that invisible enemy who defied his master's voice. By degrees, however, he quieted down, came back and stretched himself in front of the fire. But he was uneasy and kept his head up and growled between his teeth.

Ulrich, in turn, recovered his senses, but as he felt faint with terror, he went and got a bottle of brandy out of the sideboard and drank off several glasses, one after another, at a gulp. His ideas became vague, his courage revived, and a feverish glow ran through his veins.

He ate scarcely anything the next day and limited himself to alcohol; so he lived for several days, like a drunken brute. As soon as he thought of Gaspard Hari he began to drink again and went on drinking until he fell onto the floor, overcome by intoxication. And there he remained on his face, dead drunk, his limbs benumbed, and snoring with his face to the ground. But scarcely had he digested the maddening and burning liquor than the same cry, "Ulrich," woke him like a bullet piercing his brain, and he got up, still staggering, stretching out his hands to save himself from falling and calling to Sam to help him. And the dog, who appeared to be going mad like his master, rushed to the door, scratched it with claws and gnawed it with his long white teeth, while the young man, his neck thrown back and his head in the air, drank the brandy in gulps, as if it were cold water, so that it might by and by send his thoughts, his frantic terror and his memory to sleep again.

In three weeks he had consumed all his stock of ardent spirits. But his continual drunkenness only lulled his terror, which awoke more furiously than ever as soon as it was impossible for him to calm it by drinking. His fixed idea which had been intensified by a month of drunkenness and which was continually increasing in his absolute solitude penetrated him like a gimlet. He now walked about his house like a wild beast in its cage, putting his ear to the door to listen if the other were there and defying him through the wall. Then as soon as he dozed, overcome by fatigue, he heard the voice which made him leap to his feet.

At last one night, as cowards do when driven to extremity, he sprang to the door and opened it to see who was calling him and to force him to keep quiet. But such a gust of cold wind blew into his face that it chilled him to the bone. He closed and bolted the door again immediately without noticing that Sam had rushed out. Then as he was shivering with cold, he threw some wood on the fire and sat down in front of it to warm himself. But suddenly he started, for somebody was scratching at the wall and crying. In desperation he called out: "Go away!" but was answered by another long, sorrowful wail.

Then all his remaining senses forsook him from sheer fright. He repeated: "Go away!" and turned round to find some corner in which to hide, while the other person went round the house still crying and rubbing against the wall. Ulrich went to the oak sideboard which was full of plates and dishes and of provisions and, lifting it up with superhuman strength, he dragged it to the door so as to form a barricade. Then piling up all the rest of the furniture, the mattresses, paillasses and chairs, he stopped up the windows as men do when assailed by an enemy.

But the person outside now uttered long, plaintive, mournful groans, to which the young man replied by similar groans, and thus days and nights passed without their ceasing to howl at each other. The one was continually walking round the house and scraped the walls with his nails so vigorously that it seemed as if he wished to destroy them, while the other, inside, followed all his movements, stooping down and holding his ear to the walls and replying to all his appeals with terrible cries. One evening, however, Ulrich heard nothing more, and he sat down, so overcome by fatigue that he went to sleep immediately and awoke in the morning without a thought, without any recollection of what had happened, just as if his head had been emptied during his heavy sleep. But he felt hungry, and he ate.

The winter was over, and the Gemmi pass was practicable again, so Hauser family started off to return to their inn. As soon as they had reached the top of the ascent the women mounted their mule and spoke about the two men whom they would meet again shortly. They were, indeed, rather surprised that neither of them had come down a few days before, as soon the road became passable, in order to tell them all about their long winter sojourn. At last, however, they saw the inn, still covered with snow, like a quilt. The door and the windows were closed, but a little smoke was coming out of the chimney, which reassured old Hauser; on going up to the door, however, he saw the skeleton of an animal which had been torn to pieces by the eagles, a large skeleton lying on its side.

They all looked closely at it, and the mother said: "That must be Sam." Then she shouted: "Hi! Gaspard!" A cry from the interior of the house answered her, so sharp a cry that one might have thought some animal uttered it. Old Hauser repeated: "Hi! Gaspard! and they heard another cry, similar to the first.

Then the three men, the father and the two sons, tried to open the door, but it resisted their efforts. From the empty cow stall they rook a beam to serve as a battering-ram and hurled it against the door with all their might. The wood gave way, and the boards flew into splinters; then the house was shaken by a loud voice, and inside, behind the sideboard which was overturned, they saw a man standing upright, his hair falling onto his shoulders and a beard descending to his breast, with shining eyes and nothing but rags to cover him. They did not recognize him, but Louise Hauser exclaimed: "It is Ulrich, Mother." And her mother declared that it was Ulrich, although his hair was white.

He allowed them to go up to him and to touch him, but he did not reply to any of their questions, and they were obliged to take him to Loëche, where the doctors found that he was mad. Nobody ever knew what had become of his companion.

Little Louise Hauser nearly died that summer of decline, which the medical men attributed to the cold air of the mountains.

IX   The Gift of the Magi
By O. Henry

One dollar and eighty-seven cents. That was all. And sixty cents of it was in pennies. Pennies saved one and two at a time by bulldozing the grocer and the vegetable man and the butcher until one's cheeks burned with the silent imputation of parsimony that such close dealing implied. Three times Della counted it. One dollar and eighty-seven cents. And the next day would be Christmas.

There was clearly nothing to do but flop down on the shabby little couch and howl. So Della did it. Which instigates the moral reflection that life is made up of sobs, sniffles, and smiles, with sniffles predominating.

While the mistress of the home is gradually subsiding from the first stage to the second, take a look at the home. A furnished flat at $8 per week. It did not exactly beggar description, but it certainly had that word on the lookout for the mendicancy squad.

In the vestibule below was a letter-box into which no letter would go, and an electric button from which no mortal finger could coax a ring. Also appertaining thereunto was a card bearing the name "Mr. James Dillingham Young."

The "Dillingham" had been flung to the breeze during a former period of prosperity when its possessor was being paid $30 per week. Now, when the income was shrunk to $20, though, they were thinking seriously of contracting to a modest and unassuming D. But whenever Mr. James Dillingham Young came home and reached his flat above he was called "Jim" and greatly hugged by Mrs. James Dillingham Young, already introduced to you as Della. Which is all very good.

Della finished her cry and attended to her cheeks with the powder rag. She stood by the window and looked out dully at a gray cat walking a gray fence in a gray backyard. Tomorrow would be Christmas Day, and she had only $1.87 with which to buy Jim a present. She had been saving every penny she could for months, with this result. Twenty dollars a week doesn't go far. Expenses had been greater than she had calculated. They always are. Only $1.87 to buy a present for Jim. Her Jim. Many a happy hour she had spent planning for something nice for him. Something fine and rare and sterling--something just a little bit near to being worthy of the honor of being owned by Jim.

There was a pier-glass between the windows of the room. Perhaps you have seen a pier-glass in an $8 flat. A very thin and very agile person may, by observing his reflection in a rapid sequence of longitudinal strips, obtain a fairly accurate conception of his looks. Della, being slender, had mastered the art.

Suddenly she whirled from the window and stood before the glass. Her eyes were shining brilliantly, but her face had lost its color within twenty seconds. Rapidly she pulled down her hair and let it fall to its full length.

Now, there were two possessions of the James Dillingham Youngs in which they both took a mighty pride. One was Jim's gold watch that had been his father's and his grandfather's. The other was Della's hair. Had the queen of Sheba lived in the flat across the airshaft, Della would have let her hair hang out the window some day to dry just to depreciate Her Majesty's jewels and gifts. Had King Solomon been the janitor, with all his treasures piled up in the basement, Jim would have pulled out his watch every time he passed, just to see him pluck at his beard from envy.

So now Della's beautiful hair fell about her rippling and shining like a cascade of brown waters. It reached below her knee and made itself almost a garment for her. And then she did it up again nervously and quickly. Once she faltered for a minute and stood still while a tear or two splashed on the worn red carpet.

On went her old brown jacket; on went her old brown hat. With a whirl of skirts and with the brilliant sparkle still in her eyes, she fluttered out the door and down the stairs to the street.

Where she stopped the sign read: "Mme. Sofronie. Hair Goods of All Kinds." One flight up Della ran, and collected herself, panting. Madame, large, too white, chilly, hardly looked the "Sofronie."

"Will you buy my hair?" asked Della.

"I buy hair," said Madame. "Take yer hat off and let's have a sight at the looks of it."

Down rippled the brown cascade.

"Twenty dollars," said Madame, lifting the mass with a practised hand.

"Give it to me quick," said Della.

Oh, and the next two hours tripped by on rosy wings. Forget the hashed metaphor. She was ransacking the stores for Jim's present.

She found it at last. It surely had been made for Jim and no one else. There was no other like it in any of the stores, and she had turned all of them inside out. It was a platinum fob chain simple and chaste in design, properly proclaiming its value by substance alone and not by meretricious ornamentation--as all good things should do. It was even worthy of The Watch. As soon as she saw it she knew that it must be Jim's. It was like him. Quietness and value--the description applied to both. Twenty-one dollars they took from her for it, and she hurried home with the 87 cents. With that chain on his watch Jim might be properly anxious about the time in any company. Grand as the watch was, he sometimes looked at it on the sly on account of the old leather strap that he used in place of a chain.

When Della reached home her intoxication gave way a little to prudence and reason. She got out her curling irons and lighted the gas and went to work repairing the ravages made by generosity added to love. Which is always a tremendous task, dear friends--a mammoth task.

Within forty minutes her head was covered with tiny, close-lying curls that made her look wonderfully like a truant schoolboy. She looked at her reflection in the mirror long, carefully, and critically.

"If Jim doesn't kill me," she said to herself, "before he takes a second look at me, he'll say I look like a Coney Island chorus girl. But what could I do--oh! what could I do with a dollar and eighty-seven cents?"

At 7 o'clock the coffee was made and the frying-pan was on the back of the stove hot and ready to cook the chops.

Jim was never late. Della doubled the fob chain in her hand and sat on the corner of the table near the door that he always entered. Then she heard his step on the stair away down on the first flight, and she turned white for just a moment. She had a habit for saying little silent prayers about the simplest everyday things, and now she whispered: "Please God, make him think I am still pretty."

The door opened and Jim stepped in and closed it. He looked thin and very serious. Poor fellow, he was only twenty-two--and to be burdened with a family! He needed a new overcoat and he was without gloves.

Jim stopped inside the door, as immovable as a setter at the scent of quail. His eyes were fixed upon Della, and there was an expression in them that she could not read, and it terrified her. It was not anger, nor surprise, nor disapproval, nor horror, nor any of the sentiments that she had been prepared for. He simply stared at her fixedly with that peculiar expression on his face.

Della wriggled off the table and went for him.

"Jim, darling," she cried, "don't look at me that way. I had my hair cut off and sold because I couldn't have lived through Christmas without giving you a present. It'll grow out again--you won't mind, will you? I just had to do it. My hair grows awfully fast. Say 'Merry Christmas!' Jim, and let's be happy. You don't know what a nice--what a beautiful, nice gift I've got for you."

"You've cut off your hair?" asked Jim, laboriously, as if he had not arrived at that patent fact yet even after the hardest mental labor.

"Cut it off and sold it," said Della. "Don't you like me just as well, anyhow? I'm me without my hair, ain't I?"

Jim looked about the room curiously.

"You say your hair is gone?" he said, with an air almost of idiocy.

"You needn't look for it," said Della. "It's sold, I tell you--sold and gone, too. It's Christmas Eve, boy. Be good to me, for it went for you. Maybe the hairs of my head were numbered," she went on with sudden serious sweetness, "but nobody could ever count my love for you. Shall I put the chops on, Jim?"

Out of his trance Jim seemed quickly to wake. He enfolded his Della. For ten seconds let us regard with discreet scrutiny some inconsequential object in the other direction. Eight dollars a week or a million a year--what is the difference? A mathematician or a wit would give you the wrong answer. The magi brought valuable gifts, but that was not among them. This dark assertion will be illuminated later on.

Jim drew a package from his overcoat pocket and threw it upon the table.

"Don't make any mistake, Dell," he said, "about me. I don't think there's anything in the way of a haircut or a shave or a shampoo that could make me like my girl any less. But if you'll unwrap that package you may see why you had me going a while at first."

White fingers and nimble tore at the string and paper. And then an ecstatic scream of joy; and then, alas! a quick feminine change to hysterical tears and wails, necessitating the immediate employment of all the comforting powers of the lord of the flat.

For there lay The Combs--the set of combs, side and back, that Della had worshipped long in a Broadway window. Beautiful combs, pure tortoise shell, with jewelled rims--just the shade to wear in the beautiful vanished hair. They were expensive combs, she knew, and her heart had simply craved and yearned over them without the least hope of possession. And now, they were hers, but the tresses that should have adorned the coveted adornments were gone.

But she hugged them to her bosom, and at length she was able to look up with dim eyes and a smile and say: "My hair grows so fast, Jim!"

And them Della leaped up like a little singed cat and cried, "Oh, oh!"

Jim had not yet seen his beautiful present. She held it out to him eagerly upon her open palm. The dull precious metal seemed to flash with a reflection of her bright and ardent spirit.

"Isn't it a dandy, Jim? I hunted all over town to find it. You'll have to look at the time a hundred times a day now. Give me your watch. I want to see how it looks on it."

Instead of obeying, Jim tumbled down on the couch and put his hands under the back of his head and smiled.

"Dell," said he, "let's put our Christmas presents away and keep 'em a while. They're too nice to use just at present. I sold the watch to get the money to buy your combs. And now suppose you put the chops on."

The magi, as you know, were wise men--wonderfully wise men--who brought gifts to the Babe in the manger. They invented the art of giving Christmas presents. Being wise, their gifts were no doubt wise ones, possibly bearing the privilege of exchange in case of duplication. And here I have lamely related to you the uneventful chronicle of two foolish children in a flat who most unwisely sacrificed for each other the greatest treasures of their house. But in a last word to the wise of these days let it be said that of all who give gifts these two were the wisest. Of all who give and receive gifts, such as they are wisest. Everywhere they are wisest. They are the magi.[5]

---

[5] This story appeared in the collection, The Four Million, 1906

X   The Massacre of the Innocents

By Maurice Maeterlinck
Translated by
Alexander Teixeira de Mattos

IT WAS close upon supper-time, that Friday the twenty-sixth day of the month of December, when a little shepherd-lad came into Nazareth, sobbing bitterly.

Some peasants drinking ale in the Blue Lion opened the shutters to look into the village orchard and observed the child running over the snow. They saw that he was Korneliz' boy and cried from the window:

"What's the matter? Get home with you to bed!"

But he replied in terror that the Spaniards were come, that they had set fire to the farm, hanged his mother among the walnut-trees and bound his nine little sisters to the trunk of a big tree.

The peasants rushed out of the inn, gathered round the child and plied him with questions. Then he also told them that the soldiers were on horseback and wore mail, that they had driven away the cattle of his uncle Petrus Krayer and that they would soon be entering the forest with the cows and sheep.

All ran to the Golden Sun, where Korneliz and his brother-in-law were also drinking their pot of ale; and the inn-keeper sped into the village, shouting that the Spaniards were at hand.

Then there was a great din in Nazareth. The women opened the windows and the peasants left their houses with lights which they put out as soon as they reached the orchard, where it was bright as midday, because of the snow and the full moon.

They crowded round Korneliz and Krayer in the mar-

144

ket-place, in front of the two inns. Several had brought their pitchforks and their rakes and consulted one another, terror-stricken, under the trees.

But, as they knew not what to do, one of them went to fetch the parish-priest, who owned Korneliz' farm. He came out of his house with the sacristan, bringing the keys of the church. All followed him into the churchyard; and he shouted to them from the top of the tower that he could see nothing in the fields nor in the forest, but that there were red clouds in the neighbourhood of his farm, though the sky was blue and full of stars over all the rest of the country.

After deliberating for a long time in the churchyard, they decided to hide in the wood through which the Spaniards would have to pass and to attack them if they were not too many, so as to recover Petrus Krayer's cattle and the plunder which they had taken from the farm.

They armed themselves with pitchforks and spades; and the women remained near the church with the priest.

Seeking a suitable spot for their ambuscade, they came to a mill on the skirt of the forest and saw the farm burning amid the starlight. Here, under some huge oaks, in front of a frozen pool, they took up their position.

A shepherd whom they called the Red Dwarf went up the hill to warn the miller, who had stopped his mill when he saw the flames on the horizon. He invited the fellow in, however; and the two of them placed themselves at a window to watch the distance.

In front of them the moon was shining over the burning farm; and they saw a long host marching over the snow. When they had taken stock of it, the Dwarf went down to those in the forest; and presently they descried four horsemen above a herd of animals that seemed to be cropping the grass.

As the men, in their blue hose and their red cloaks, were looking around them on the edge of the pool and under the snow-lit trees, the sacristan pointed to a box-hedge; and they went and hid behind it.

The cattle and the Spaniards came over the ice; and the sheep on reaching the hedge were already beginning to nibble at the leaves, when Korneliz broke through the bushes; and the others followed with their pitchforks into the light. Then there was a great slaughter on the pond, while the huddled sheep and the cows gazed at the battle in their midst and at the moon above them.

When the men and the horses had been killed, Korneliz ran into the meadows towards the flames; and the others stripped the dead. Then they went back to the village with the herds. The women watching the gloomy forest from behind the walls of the churchyard saw them approaching through the trees and, with the priest, hurried to meet them; and they returned dancing gleefully all amongst the children and the dogs.

While they made merry under the pear-trees in the orchard, where the Red Dwarf hung up lanterns as a sign of kermis, they consulted the priest as to what they were to do.

They at last resolved to put a horse to a cart and fetch the bodies of the woman and her nine little daughters to the village. The dead woman's sisters and the other peasant-women of her family climbed into it, as did the priest, who was not well able to walk, being advanced in years and very stout.

They entered the forest once more and arrived in silence at the dazzling white plain, where they saw the naked men and the horses lying on their backs upon the gleaming ice among the trees. Then they went on to the farm, which they could see burning in the distance.

When they came to the orchard and to the house all red with flames, they stopped at the gate to mark the great misfortune that had befallen the farmer in his garden. His wife was hanging all naked from the branches of a great walnut-tree; he himself was mounting a ladder to climb the tree, around which the nine little girls were waiting for their mother on the grass. Already he was walking among the huge boughs, when suddenly he saw the crowd, black against the snow, watching him. Weeping, he made signs to them to help him; and they went into the garden. Then the sacristan, the Red Dwarf, the landlord of the Blue Lion and he of the Golden Sun, the parish-priest, with a lantern, and many other peasants climbed into the snow-laden walnut-tree to cut down the corpse, which the women of the village received in their arms at the foot of the tree, even as at the descent from the Cross of Our Lord Jesus Christ.

The next day they buried her; and nothing else out of the common happened at Nazareth that week. But, on the following Sunday, hungry wolves ran through the village after high mass and it snowed until noon; then the sun suddenly shone in the sky; and the peasants went in to dinner, as was their wont, and dressed for benediction.

At that moment there was no one in the market-place, for it was freezing cruelly. Only the dogs and hens remained under the trees, where some sheep were nibbling at a three-cornered patch of grass, while the priest's maidservant swept away the snow from the presbytery-garden.

Then a troop of armed men crossed the stone bridge at the end of the village and halted in the orchard. Some peasants came out of their houses; but, on recognizing the

Spaniards, they retreated in terror and went to their windows to see what would happen.

There were some thirty horsemen, clad in armour, around an old man with a white beard. Behind them they carried red and yellow foot-soldiers, who jumped down and ran over the snow to shake oft their stiffness, while several of the men in armour also alighted and eased themselves against the trees to which they had fastened their horses.

Then they turned to the Golden Sun and knocked at the door. It was opened hesitatingly; and they warmed themselves at the fire and called for ale.

Next they came out of the inn, carrying pots and jugs and wheaten loaves for their comrades, who sat ranked around the man with the white beard, waiting in the midst of the lances.

As the street was empty, the commander sent horsemen to the back of the houses, to guard the village on its open side, and ordered the foot-soldiers to bring to him all the children of two years old and under, to be massacred, as is written in the Gospel according to St. Matthew.

The soldiers went first to the inn of the Green Cabbage and to the barber's cottage, which stood side by side, midway in the street.

One of them opened a stable-door; and a litter of pigs escaped and scattered over the village. The inn-keeper and the barber came out and humbly asked the soldiers what they wanted; but the men knew no Flemish and went in to look for the children.

The inn-keeper had one, which sat crying in its little shirt on the table where they had just had dinner. A man took the child in his arms and carried it away under the apple-tree, while the father and mother followed him with cries of lamentation.

The soldiers also threw open the cooper's shed and the blacksmith's and the cobbler's; and the calves, cows, asses, pigs, goats and sheep strayed about the marketplace. When the men broke the glass of the carpenter's windows, several of the peasants, including the oldest and richest farmers in the parish, assembled in the street and went towards the Spaniards. They doffed their hats and caps respectfully to the leader in his velvet cloak and asked him what he was going to do; but even he did not understand their language; and some one went to fetch the priest.

He was making ready for benediction and putting on a gold cope in the sacristy. The peasant called out:

"The Spaniards are in the orchard!"

Horrified, the priest ran to the church-door, accompanied by the serving-boys carrying tapers and censer.

Then he saw the animals released from their sheds roaming on the snow and the grass, the horsemen in the village, the soldiers outside the doors, the horses tied to the trees along the street and the men and women entreating him who was holding the child in its shirt.

He rushed to the churchyard; and the peasants turned anxiously to their priest, coming through the pear-trees like a god robed in gold, and stood around him and the man with the white beard.

He spoke in Flemish and Latin; but the commander shrugged his shoulders slowly up and down to show that he did not understand.

His parishioners asked him under their breath:

"What does he say? What is he going to do?"

Others, on seeing the priest in the orchard, came timidly from their farms; the women hurried up and stood whispering among the groups; while some soldiers who were

149

besieging an inn ran back at the sight of the great crowd that was forming in the market-place.

Then the man who was holding by one leg the child of the landlord of the Green Cabbage cut off its head with his sword.

The head fell before their eyes and the body fell after it and lay bleeding on the grass. The mother picked it up and carried it away, leaving the head behind her. She ran towards the house, but stumbled against a tree and fell flat on the snow, where she lay in a swoon, while the father struggled between two soldiers.

Some of the younger peasants threw stones and blocks of wood at the Spaniards, but the horsemen all lowered their lances together, the women fled and the priest began to cry out in horror with his parishioners, all among the sheep, the geese and the dogs.

However, as the soldiers were once more moving down the street, the folk stood silent to see what they would do.

The band entered the shop kept by the sacristan's sisters and then came out quietly, without harming the seven women, who knelt on the doorstep praying.

Next they went to the inn owned by the Hunchback of St. Nicholas. Here also the door was opened directly, to appease them; but they reappeared amid a great outcry, with three children in their arms and surrounded by the Hunchback, his wife and his daughters, clasping their hands in token of entreaty.

On reaching the old man, the soldiers put down the children at the foot of an elm, where they remained, sitting on the snow in their Sunday clothes. But one of them, who wore a yellow frock, rose and toddled towards the sheep. A man ran after it with his naked sword; and the child died with its face in the grass, while the others were killed not far from the tree.

All the peasants and the inn-keeper's daughters took to flight, shrieking as they went, and returned to their homes. The priest, left alone in the orchard, besought the Spaniards with loud cries, going on his knees from horse to horse, with his arms crossed upon his breast, while the father and mother, sitting in the snow, wept piteously for the dead children that lay in their laps.

As the soldiers ran along the street, they remarked a big blue farm-house. They tried to break down the door, but it was of oak and studded with nails. Then they took some tubs that were frozen in a pool in front of the house and used them to climb to the upper windows, through which they made their way.

There had been a kermis at this farm; and kinsfolk had come to eat waffles, ham and custards with their family. At the sound of the broken panes, they had assembled behind the table covered with jugs and dishes. The soldiers entered the kitchen and, after a desperate struggle, in which many were wounded, they seized the little boys and girls, as well as the hind, who had bitten a soldier's thumb. Then they left the house, locking the door behind them to prevent the inmates from going with them.

Those of the villagers who had no children slowly left their homes and followed them from afar. When the soldiers carrying their victims came to the old man, they threw them on the grass and deliberately killed them with their spears and their swords, while all along the front of the blue house the men and women leant out of the windows of the upper floor and the loft, cursing and rocking wildly in the sunshine at the sight of the red, pink and white frocks of their little ones lying motionless on the grass among the trees. Then the soldiers hanged the hind from the sign of the Half Moon on the other side of the street; and there was a long silence in the village.

The massacre now began to spread. Mothers ran out of the houses and tried to escape to the open country through the gardens and kitchen-plots; but the horsemen scoured after them and drove them back into the street. Peasants, holding their caps in their clasped hands, followed upon their knees the men who were dragging away their children, among the dogs which barked deliriously amid the din. The priest, with his arms raised aloft, ran along the houses and under the trees, praying desperately, like a martyr; and soldiers, shivering with cold, blew on their fingers as they moved about the road, or, with their hands in the pockets of their trunks and their swords tucked under their arms, waited beneath the windows of the houses that were being scaled.

On seeing the grief-stricken terror of the peasants, they entered the farm-houses in little bands; and in like fashion they acted throughout the length of the street.

A woman who sold vegetables in the old red-brick cottage near the church seized a chair and ran after two men who were carrying off her children in a wheel-barrow. When she saw them die, a sickness overcame her; and she suffered the folk to press her into the chair, against a tree by the road-side.

Other soldiers climbed up the lime-trees in front of a house painted lilac and removed the tiles in order to enter the house. When they came out again upon the roof, the father and mother, with outstretched arms, also appeared in the opening; and they pushed them down repeatedly, cutting them over the head with their swords, before they could descend into the street.

One family, which had locked itself into the cellar of a

rambling cottage, cried through the grating, where the father stood madly brandishing a pitchfork. An old, bald-headed man was sobbing all alone on a dung-heap; a woman in yellow had fainted in the market-place and her husband was holding her under her arms and moaning in the shadow of a pear-tree; another, in red, was kissing her little girl, who had lost her hands, and lifting first one arm and then the other to see if she would not move. Yet another ran into the country and the soldiers pursued her through the hayricks that bounded the snow-clad fields.

Beneath the inn of the Four Sons of Aymon there was a tumult as of a siege. The inhabitants had barred the door; and the soldiers went round and round the house without being able to make their way in. They were trying to clamber up to the sign by the fruit-trees against the front wall, when they caught sight of a ladder behind the garden-door. They set it against the wall and mounted one after the other. Thereupon the landlord and all his household hurled tables, chairs, dishes and cradles at them from the windows. The ladder upset and the soldiers fell down.

In a wooden hut, at the end of the village, another band found a peasant-woman bathing her children in a tub by the fire. Being old and almost deaf, she did not hear them come in. Two soldiers took the tub and carried it off; and the dazed woman went after them, with the children's clothes, wanting to dress them. But, when she came to the door and suddenly saw the splashes of blood in the village, the swords in the orchard, the cradles overturned in the street, women on their knees and women waving their arms around the dead, she began to cry out with all her strength and to strike the soldiers, who put down the tub to defend themselves. The priest also came hastening up and, folding his hands across his vestment, entreated the

Spaniards before the naked children, who were whimpering in the water. Other soldiers then came up and pushed him aside and bound the raving peasant-woman to a tree.

The butcher had hidden his little daughter and, leaning against his house, looked on in unconcern. A foot-soldier and one of the men in armour went in and discovered the child in a copper cauldron. Then the butcher, in desperation, took one of his knives and chased them down the street; but a band that was passing struck the knife from his grasp and hanged him by the hands to the hooks in his wall, among the flayed carcases, where he twitched his legs and jerked his head and cursed and swore till evening.

Near the churchyard, a crowd had assembled outside a long green farm-house. The farmer stood on his threshold weeping bitter tears; as he was very fat, with a face made for smiling, the hearts of the soldiers softened in some measure as they sat in the sun with their backs to the wall, listening to him and patting his dog the while. But the one who was dragging the child away by the hand made gestures as though to say:

"You may save your tears! It is not my fault!"

A peasant who was being hotly pursued sprang into a boat moored to the stone bridge and pushed across the pond with his wife and children. The soldiers, not daring to venture on the ice, strode angrily through the reeds. They climbed into the willows on the bank, trying to reach them with their spears; and, when they failed, continued for a long time to threaten the family, where they all sat cowering in the middle of the water.

Meanwhile, the orchard was still full of people, for it was there that most of the children were slain, in front of the man with the white beard who directed the massacre.

The little boys and girls who were big enough to walk alone also collected there and, munching their bread-and-butter, stood looking on curiously to see the others die or gathered round the village idiot, who lay upon the grass playing a whistle.

Then suddenly a movement ran through the length of the village. The peasants were turning their steps toward the castle, standing on a high mound of yellow earth at the end of the street. They had caught sight of the lord of the village leaning on the battlements of his tower, watching the massacre. And the men, women and old folk stretched out their arms to him where he sat in his cloak of purple velvet and cap of gold and entreated him as though he were a king in heaven. But he threw up his arms and shrugged his shoulders, to show his helplessness; and, when they implored him in ever-increasing anguish and knelt bareheaded in the snow, uttering loud cries, he turned back slowly into the tower; and in the hearts of the peasants all hope died.

When all the children were killed, the tired soldiers wiped their swords on the grass and supped under the pear-trees. Then the foot-soldiers mounted behind the others and they all rode out of Nazareth together, by the stone bridge, as they had come.

The setting sun lit the forest with a red light and painted the village a new colour. Weary with running and entreating, the priest had sat down in the snow in front of the church; and his servant-maid stood near him, looking around. They saw the street and the orchard filled with peasants in their holiday attire, moving about the market-place and along the houses. Outside the doors, families, with their dead children on their knees, whispered in amazement and horror of the fate wherewith they had been assailed. Others were still mourning the child where it had fallen, near a cask, under a barrow or at a puddle's edge, or were carrying it away in silence. Several were already washing the benches, chairs, tables and shirts all smirched with blood and picking up the cradles that had been flung into the street. But nearly all the mothers were kneeling on the grass under the trees, before the dead bodies, which they knew by their woollen frocks. Those who had no children were roaming about the market-place, stopping to gaze at the afflicted groups. The men who had done weeping took the dogs and started in pursuit of their strayed beasts, or mended their broken windows or gaping roofs, while the village grew hushed and still beneath the light of the moon as it rose slowly in the sky.[6]

[Author's note:] The Massacre of the Innocents appeared for the first time in 1886, in a little periodical called La Pléiade which some friends and I had founded in the Latin Quarter and which died of inanition after its sixth number. My reason for making room in the present volume for these pages marking a very modest start--they were the first that found their way into print--is not that I am under any delusion as to the merits of this youthful work, in which I had simply aimed at reproducing as best I could the different episodes of a picture in the Brussels Museum painted in the sixteenth century by Pieter Breughel the Elder. But it appeared to me that circumstances had made of this humble literary effort a sort of prophetic vision, for it is but too likely that similar scenes

---

[6] From The Wrack of the Storm
Copyright 1916, Dodd, Mead, and Company

must have been repeated in more than one of our unhappy Flemish or Brabant villages and that to describe them as they were lately enacted we should have only to change the name of the butchers and probably, alas, to accentuate their cruelty, their injustice and their hideousness!----M. M.

[Translator's note:] The present volume [The Wrack of the Storm] contains, in the chronological order in which they were produced, all the essays published and all the speeches delivered by M. Maeterlinck since the beginning of the war [World War I]. . . . I have also had M. Maeterlinck's leave to include in this volume his first published work, The Massacre of the Innocents. This powerful sketch in the Flemish manner saw the light originally in the Pléiade, in 1886, and may at the present time, to use the author's own words in a note to myself, be regarded as "a sort of vague symbolic prophecy." An English version by Mrs. Edith Wingate Rinder was printed in the Dome in 1899; another has since been issued by an English and by an American firm of publishers; but the only authorized translation to appear in book form is that now added as an epilogue to The Wrack of the Storm. [pages 303-330]
--Alexander Teixeira de Mattos

Chelsea, 1916.

XI Misery

By Anton Chekhov

THE twilight of evening. Big flakes of wet snow are whirling lazily about the street lamps, which have just been lighted, and lying in a thin soft layer on roofs, horses' backs, shoulders, caps. Iona Potapov, the sledge-driver, is all white like a ghost. He sits on the box without stirring, bent as double as the living body can be bent. If a regular snowdrift fell on him it seems as though even then he would not think it necessary to shake it off. . . . His little mare is white and motionless too. Her stillness, the angularity of her lines, and the stick-like straightness of her legs make her look like a halfpenny gingerbread horse. She is probably lost in thought. Anyone who has been torn away from the plough, from the familiar gray landscapes, and cast into this slough, full of monstrous lights, of unceasing uproar and hurrying people, is bound to think.

It is a long time since Iona and his nag have budged. They came out of the yard before dinnertime and not a single fare yet. But now the shades of evening are falling on the town. The pale light of the street lamps changes to a vivid color, and the bustle of the street grows noisier.

"Sledge to Vyborgskaya!" Iona hears. "Sledge!"

Iona starts, and through his snow-plastered eyelashes sees an officer in a military overcoat with a hood over his head.

"To Vyborgskaya," repeats the officer. "Are you asleep? To Vyborgskaya!"

In token of assent Iona gives a tug at the reins which sends cakes of snow flying from the horse's back and shoulders. The officer gets into the sledge. The sledge-driver clicks to the horse, cranes his neck like a swan, rises in his seat, and more from habit than necessity brandishes his whip. The mare cranes her neck, too, crooks her stick-like legs, and hesitatingly sets off. . . .

"Where are you shoving, you devil?" Iona immediately hears shouts from the dark mass shifting to and fro before him. "Where the devil are you going? Keep to the r-right!"

"You don't know how to drive! Keep to the right," says the officer angrily.

A coachman driving a carriage swears at him; a pedestrian crossing the road and brushing the horse's nose with his shoulder looks at him angrily and shakes the snow off his sleeve. Iona fidgets on the box as though he were sitting on thorns, jerks his elbows, and turns his eyes about like one possessed as though he did not know where he was or why he was there.

"What rascals they all are!" says the officer jocosely. "They are simply doing their best to run up against you or fall under the horse's feet. They must be doing it on purpose."

Iona looks as his fare and moves his lips. . . . Apparently he means to say something, but nothing comes but a sniff.

"What?" inquires the officer.

Iona gives a wry smile, and straining his throat, brings out huskily: "My son . . . er . . . my son died this week, sir."

"H'm! What did he die of?"

Iona turns his whole body round to his fare, and says:

"Who can tell! It must have been from fever. . . . He lay three days in the hospital and then he died. . . . God's will."

"Turn round, you devil!" comes out of the darkness. "Have you gone cracked, you old dog? Look where you are going!"

"Drive on! drive on! . . ." says the officer. "We shan't get there till to-morrow going on like this. Hurry up!"

159

The sledge-driver cranes his neck again, rises in his seat, and with heavy grace swings his whip. Several times he looks round at the officer, but the latter keeps his eyes shut and is apparently disinclined to listen. Putting his fare down at Vyborgskaya, Iona stops by a restaurant, and again sits huddled up on the box. . . . Again the wet snow paints him and his horse white. One hour passes, and then another. . . .

Three young men, two tall and thin, one short and hunchbacked, come up, railing at each other and loudly stamping on the pavement with their goloshes.

"Cabby, to the Police Bridge!" the hunchback cries in a cracked voice. "The three of us, . . . twenty kopecks!"

Iona tugs at the reins and clicks to his horse. Twenty kopecks is not a fair price, but he has no thoughts for that. Whether it is a rouble or whether it is five kopecks does not matter to him now so long as he has a fare. . . . The three young men, shoving each other and using bad language, go up to the sledge, and all three try to sit down at once. The question remains to be settled: Which are to sit down and which one is to stand? After a long altercation, ill-temper, and abuse, they come to the conclusion that the hunchback must stand because he is the shortest.

"Well, drive on," says the hunchback in his cracked voice, settling himself and breathing down Iona's neck. "Cut along! What a cap you've got, my friend! You wouldn't find a worse one in all Petersburg. . . ."

"He-he! . . . he-he! . . ." laughs Iona. "It's nothing to boast of!"

"Well, then, nothing to boast of, drive on! Are you going to drive like this all the way? Eh? Shall I give you one in the neck?"

"My head aches," says one of the tall ones. "At the

Dukmasovs' yesterday Vaska and I drank four bottles of brandy between us."

"I can't make out why you talk such stuff," says the other tall one angrily. "You lie like a brute."

"Strike me dead, it's the truth! . . ."

"It's about as true as that a louse coughs."

"He-he!" grins Iona. "Me-er-ry gentlemen!"

"Tfoo! the devil take you!" cries the hunchback indignantly. "Will you get on, you old plague, or won't you? Is that the way to drive? Give her one with the whip. Hang it all, give it her well."

Iona feels behind his back the jolting person and quivering voice of the hunchback. He hears abuse addressed to him, he sees people, and the feeling of loneliness begins little by little to be less heavy on his heart. The hunchback swears at him, till he chokes over some elaborately whimsical string of epithets and is overpowered by his cough. His tall companions begin talking of a certain Nadyezhda Petrovna. Iona looks round at them. Waiting till there is a brief pause, he looks round once more and says:

"This week . . . er. . . my. . . er. . . son died!"

"We shall all die, . . ." says the hunchback with a sigh, wiping his lips after coughing. "Come, drive on! drive on! My friends, I simply cannot stand crawling like this! When will he get us there?"

"Well, you give him a little encouragement . . . one in the neck!"

"Do you hear, you old plague? I'll make you smart. If one stands on ceremony with fellows like you one may as well walk. Do you hear, you old dragon? Or don't you care a hang what we say? "

And Iona hears rather than feels a slap on the back of his neck.

161

"He-he! . . . " he laughs. "Merry gentlemen . . . . God give you health!"

"Cabman, are you married?" asks one of the tall ones.

"I? He he! Me-er-ry gentlemen. The only wife for me now is the damp earth. .. . . He-ho-ho!. . . .The grave that is! . . . Here my son's dead and I am alive. . . . It's a strange thing, death has come in at the wrong door. .. . .. Instead of coming for me it went for my son. . . ."

And Iona turns round to tell them how his son died, but at that point the hunchback gives a faint sigh and announces that, thank God! they have arrived at last. After taking his twenty kopecks, Iona gazes for a long while after the revelers, who disappear into a dark entry. Again he is alone and again there is silence for him. . . . The misery which has been for a brief space eased comes back again and tears his heart more cruelly than ever. With a look of anxiety and suffering Iona's eyes stray restlessly among the crowds moving to and fro on both sides of the street: can he not find among those thousands someone who will listen to him? But the crowds flit by heedless of him and his misery. . . . His misery is immense, beyond all bounds. If Iona's heart were to burst and his misery to flow out, it would flood the whole world, it seems, but yet it is not seen. It has found a hiding-place in such an insignificant shell that one would not have found it with a candle by daylight. . . .

Iona sees a house-porter with a parcel and makes up his mind to address him.

"What time will it be, friend?" he asks.

"Going on for ten. . . . Why have you stopped here? Drive on!"

Iona drives a few paces away, bends himself double, and gives himself up to his misery. He feels it is no good to appeal to people. But before five minutes have passed he draws himself up, shakes his head as though he feels a sharp pain, and tugs at the reins. . . . He can bear it no longer.

"Back to the yard!" he thinks. "To the yard!"

And his little mare, as though she knew his thoughts, falls to trotting. An hour and a half later Iona is sitting by a big dirty stove. On the stove, on the floor, and on the benches are people snoring. The air is full of smells and stuffiness. Iona looks at the sleeping figures, scratches himself, and regrets that he has come home so early. . . .

"I have not earned enough to pay for the oats, even," he thinks. "That's why I am so miserable. A man who knows how to do his work, . . . who has had enough to eat, and whose horse has had enough to eat, is always at ease. . . ."

In one of the corners a young cabman gets up, clears his throat sleepily, and makes for the water-bucket.

"Want a drink?" Iona asks him.

"Seems so."

"May it do you good. . . . But my son is dead, mate. . . . Do you hear? This week in the hospital. . . . It's a queer business. . . ."

Iona looks to see the effect produced by his words, but he sees nothing. The young man has covered his head over and is already asleep. The old man sighs and scratches himself. . . . Just as the young man had been thirsty for water, he thirsts for speech. His son will soon have been dead a week, and he has not really talked to anybody yet . . . . He wants to talk of it properly, with deliberation. . . . He wants to tell how his son was taken ill, how he suffered, what he said before he died, how he died. . . . He wants to describe the funeral, and how he went to the hospital to get his son's clothes. He still has his daughter Anisya in the country. . . . And he wants to talk about her too. . . . Yes, he has plenty to talk about now. His listener ought to sigh and exclaim and lament. . . . It would be even better to talk to women. Though they are silly creatures, they blubber at the first word.

"Let's go out and have a look at the mare," Iona thinks. "There is always time for sleep. . . . You'll have sleep enough, no fear. . . ."

He puts on his coat and goes into the stables where his mare is standing. He thinks about oats, about hay, about the weather. . . . He cannot think about his son when he is alone. . . . To talk about him with someone is possible, but to think of him and picture him is insufferable anguish. . . .

"Are you munching?" Iona asks his mare, seeing her shining eyes. "There, munch away, munch away. . . . Since we have not earned enough for oats, we will eat hay. . . . Yes, . . . I have grown too old to drive. . . . My son ought to be driving, not I. . . . He was a real cabman. . . . He ought to have lived. . . ."

Iona is silent for a while, and then he goes on:

"That's how it is, old girl. . . . Kuzma Ionitch is gone. . . . He said good-by to me. . . . He went and died for no reason. . . . Now, suppose you had a little colt, and you were own mother to that little colt. . . . And all at once that same little colt went and died. . . . You'd be sorry, wouldn't you? . . ."

The little mare munches, listens, and breathes on her master's hands. Iona is carried away and tells her all about it.

Figure 1 "To whom shall I tell my grief?"[78]

[7] by T. Shishmarevoi from a Russian edition of "Motley Stories".
Translation by Constance Garnett, The Schoolmistress and Other
Stories, 1921, Macmillan Publishing Company.

[8] The oral poem of the 15-17th century, "Joseph's Lament", in *Spritual Verse*.

XII How Santa Claus Came to Simpson's Bar

By Bret Harte

IT had been raining in the valley of the Sacramento, the North Fork had overflowed its banks, and Rattlesnake Creek was impassable. The few boulders that had marked the summer ford at Simpson's Crossing were obliterated by a vast sheet of water stretching to the foothills. The up-stage was stopped at Granger's; the last mail had been abandoned in the *tules*, the rider swimming for his life. "An area," remarked the "Sierra Avalanche," with pensive local pride, "as large as the State of Massachusetts is now under water."

Nor was the weather any better in the foothills. The mud lay deep on the mountain road; wagons that neither physical force nor moral objurgation could move from the evil ways into which they had fallen encumbered the track, and the way to Simpson's Bar was indicated by broken-down teams and hard swearing. And further on, cut off and inaccessible, rained upon and bedraggled, smitten by high winds and threatened by high water, Simpson's Bar, on the eve of Christmas Day, 1862, clung like a swallow's nest to the rocky entablature and splintered capitals of Table Mountain, and shook in the blast.

As night shut down on the settlement, a few lights gleamed through the mist from the windows of cabins on either side of the highway, now crossed and gullied by lawless streams and swept by marauding winds. Happily most of the population were gathered at Thompson's store, clustered around a redhot stove, at which they silently spat in some accepted sense of social communion

167

that perhaps rendered conversation unnecessary. Indeed, most methods of diversion had long since been exhausted on Simpson's Bar; high water had suspended the regular occupations on gulch and on river, and a consequent lack of money and whiskey had taken the zest from most illegitimate recreation. Even Mr. Hamlin was fain to leave the Bar with fifty dollars in his pocket--the only amount actually realized of the large sums won by him in the successful exercise of his arduous profession. "Ef I was asked," he remarked somewhat later,--" ef I was asked to pint out a purty little village where a retired sport as didn't care for money could exercise hisself, frequent and lively, I'd say Simpson's Bar but for a young man with a large family depending on his exertions, it don't pay." As Mr. Hamlin's family consisted mainly of female adults, this remark is quoted rather to show the breadth of his humor than the exact extent of his responsibilities.

Howbeit, the unconscious objects of this satire sat that evening in the listless apathy begotten of idleness and lack of excitement, Even the sudden splashing of hoofs before the door did not arouse them. Dick Bullen alone paused in the act of scraping out his pipe, and lifted his head, but no other one of the group indicated any interest in, or recognition of, the man who entered.

It was a figure familiar enough to the company, and known in Simpson's Bar as "The Old Man." A man of perhaps fifty years; grizzled and scant of hair, but still fresh and youthful of complexion. A face full of ready but not very powerful sympathy, with a chameleon-like aptitude for taking on the shade and color of contiguous moods and feelings. He had evidently just left some hilarious companions, and did not at first notice the gravity of the group, but clapped the shoulder of the nearest man jocularly, and threw himself into a vacant chair "Jest heard the best thing out, boys! Ye know Smiley, over yar--Jim Smiley--funniest man in the Bar? Well, Jim was jest telling the richest yarn about"--

"Smiley's a ---- fool," interrupted a gloomy voice.

" A particular ---- skunk," added another in sepulchral accents.

A silence followed these positive statements. The Old Man glanced quickly around the group. Then his face slowly changed. "That's so," he said reflectively, after a pause, "certainly a sort of a skunk and suthin' of a fool. In course." He was silent for a moment, as in painful contemplation of the unsavoriness and folly of the unpopular Smiley. "Dismal weather, ain't it?" he added, now fully embarked on the current of prevailing sentiment. "Mighty rough papers on the boys, and no show for money this season. And to-morrow's Christmas."

There was a movement among the men at this announcement, but whether of satisfaction or disgust was not plain. "Yes," continued the Old Man in the lugubrious tone he had, within the last few moments, unconsciously adopted,-- "yes, Christmas, and to-night's Christmas Eve. Ye see, boys, I kinder thought--that is, I sorter had an idee, jest passin' like, you know-- that maybe ye'd all like to come over to my house to-night and have a sort of tear round. But I suppose, now, you wouldn't? Don't feel like it, maybe?" he added with anxious sympathy, peering into the faces of his companions.

"Well, I don't know," responded Tom Flynn with some cheerfulness. "P'r'aps we may. But how about your wife, Old Man? What does she say to it?"

The Old Man hesitated. His conjugal experience had not been a happy one, and the fact was known to Simpson's

Bar. His first wife, a delicate, pretty little woman, had. suffered keenly and secretly from the jealous suspicions of her husband, until one day he invited the whole Bar to his house to expose her infidelity. On arriving, the party found the shy, petite creature quietly engaged in her household duties, and retired abashed and discomfited. But the sensitive woman did not easily recover from the shock of this extraordinary outrage. It was with difficulty she regained her equanimity sufficiently to release her lover from the closet in which he was concealed, and escape with him. She left a boy of three years to comfort her bereaved husband. The Old Man's present wife had been his cook. She was large, loyal, and aggressive.

Before he could reply, Joe Dimmick suggested with great directness that it was the "Old Man's house," and that, invoking the Divine Power, if the case were his own, he would invite whom he pleased, even if in so doing he imperiled his salvation. The Powers of Evil, he further remarked, should contend against him vainly. All this delivered with a terseness and vigor lost in this necessary translation.

"In course. Certainly. Thet's it," said the Old Man with a sympathetic frown. "Thar's no trouble about thet, It's my own house, built every stick on it myself. Don't you be afeard o' her, boys. She may cut up a trifle rough--ez wimmin do--but she'll come round." Secretly the Old Man trusted to the exaltation of liquor and the power of courageous example to sustain him in such an emergency.

As yet, Dick Bullen, the oracle and leader of Simpson's Bar, had not spoken, He now took his pipe from his lips. "Old Man, how's that yer Johnny gettin' on? Seems to me he didn't look so peart last time I seed him on the bluff heavin' rocks at Chinamen. Didn't seem to take much in-

terest in it. Thar was a gang of 'em. by yar yesterday--
drownded out up the river--and I kinder thought o'
Johnny, and how he'd miss 'em! Maybe now, we'd be in
the way ef he wus sick?"

The father, evidently touched not only by this pathetic
picture of Johnny's deprivation, but by the considerate
delicacy of the speaker, hastened to assure him that
Johnny was better, and that a "little fun might 'liven him
up." Whereupon Dick arose, shook himself, and saying,
"I'm ready. Lead the way, Old Man: here goes," himself led
the way with a leap, a characteristic howl, and darted out
into the night. As he passed through the outer room he
caught up a blazing brand from the hearth. The action was
repeated by the rest of the party, closely following and el-
bowing each other, and before the astonished proprietor of
Thompson's grocery was aware of the intention of his
guests, the room was deserted.

The night was pitchy dark. In the first gust of wind their
temporary torches were extinguished, and only the red
brands dancing and flitting in the gloom like drunken
will-o'-the-wisps indicated their whereabouts. Their way
led up Pine-Tree Canon, at the head of which a broad, low,
bark-thatched cabin burrowed in the mountain-side. It
was the home of the Old Man, and the entrance to the tunnel in which he worked when he worked at all. Here the
crowd paused for a moment, out of delicate deference to
their host, who came up panting in the rear.

"P'r'aps ye'd better hold on a second out yer, whilst I go
in and see that things is all right," said the Old Man, with
an indifference he was far from feeling. The suggestion
was graciously accepted, the door opened and closed on
the host, and the crowd, leaning their backs against the
wall and cowering under the eaves, waited and listened,

For a few moments there was no sound but the dripping of water from the eaves, and the stir and rustle of wrestling boughs above them., Then the men became uneasy, and whispered suggestion and suspicion passed from the one to the other. "Reckon she's caved in his head the first lick!" "Decoyed him inter the tunnel and barred him up, likely" "Got him down and sittin' on him." "Prob'ly biling suthin' to heave on us: stand clear the door, boys!" For just then the latch clicked, the door slowly opened, and a voice said, "Come in out o' the wet."

The voice was neither that of the Old Man nor of his wife. It was the voice of a small boy, its weak treble broken by that preternatural hoarseness which only vagabondage and the habit of premature self-assertion can give. It was the face of a small boy that looked up at theirs,--a face that might have been pretty, and even refined, but that it was darkened by evil knowledge from within, and dirt and bard experience from without. He had a blanket around his shoulders, and had evidently just risen from his bed. "Come in," he repeated, "and don't make no noise. The Old Man's in there talking to mar," he continued, pointing to an adjacent room which seemed to be a kitchen, from which the Old Man's voice came in deprecating ac cents. "Let me be," he added querulously, to Dick Bullen, who had caught him up, blanket and all, and was affecting to toss him into the fire, "let go o' me, you d----d old fool, d' ye hear?"

Thus adjured, Dick Bullen lowered Johnny to the ground with a smothered laugh, while the men, entering quietly, ranged themselves around a long table of rough boards which occupied the centre of the room. Johnny then gravely proceeded to a cupboard and brought out several articles, which he deposited on the table. "Thar's

whiskey. And crackers. And red herons. And cheese." He
took a bite of the latter on his way to the table. "And
sugar." He scooped up a mouthful en route with a small
and very dirty hand. "And terbacker, Thar's dried appils
too on the shelf, but I don't admire'em. Appils is swellin'.
Thar," he concluded, "now wade in, and don't be afeard. I
don't mind the old woman. She don't b'long to *me*. S'long."

He had stepped to the threshold of a small room,
scarcely larger than a closet, partitioned off from the main
apartment, and holding in its dim recess a small bed. He
stood there a moment looking at the company, his bare
feet peeping from the blanket, and nodded.

"Hello, Johnny! You ain't goin' to turn in agin, are ye?"
said Dick.

"Yes, I are," responded Johnny decidedly1

"Why, wot's up, old fellow?"

"I'm sick."

"How sick?"

"I've got a fevier. And childblains. And roomatiz," returned Johnny, and vanished within. After a moment's
pause, he added in the dark, apparently from under the
bedclothes, --"And biles!"

There was an embarrassing silence. The men looked at
each other and at the fire. Even with the appetizing banquet before them, it seemed as if they might again fall into
the despondency of Thompson's grocery, when the voice
of the Old Man, incautiously lifted, came deprecatingly
from the kitchen.

"Certainly! Thet's so. In course they is. A gang o' lazy,
drunken loafers, and that ar Dick Bullen's the orneriest of
all. Didn't hev no more *sabe* than to come round yar with
sickness in the house and no provision. Thet's what I said:
'Bullen,' sez I, 'it's crazy drunk you are, 'r a fool,' sez I, 'to

173

think o' such a thing.' 'Staples,' I sez, 'be you a man, Staples, and 'spect to raise h--ll under my roof and invalids lyin' round?' But they would come,--they would. Thet's wot you must 'spect o' such trash as lays round the Bar."

A burst of laughter from the men followed this unfortunate exposure. Whether it was overheard in the kitchen, or whether the Old Man's irate companion had just then exhausted all other modes of expressing her contemptuous indignation, I cannot say, but a back door was suddenly slammed with great violence. A moment later and the Old Man reappeared, haply unconscious of the cause of the late hilarious outburst, and smiled blandly.

"The old woman thought she'd jest run over to Mrs. MacFadden's for a sociable call," he explained with jaunty indifference, as he took a seat at the board.

Oddly enough it needed this untoward incident to relieve the embarrassment that was beginning to be felt by the party, and their natural audacity returned with their host. I do not propose to record the convivialities of that evening. The inquisitive reader will accept the statement that the conversation was characterized by the same intellectual exaltation, the same cautious reverence, the same fastidious delicacy, the same rhetorical precision, and the same logical and coherent discourse somewhat later in the evening, which distinguish similar gatherings of the masculine sex in more civilized localities and under more favorable auspices. No glasses were broken in the absence of any; no liquor was uselessly spilt on the floor or table in the scarcity of that article.

It was nearly midnight when the festivities were interrupted. "Hush," said Dick Bullen, holding up his hand. It was the querulous voice of Johnny from his adjacent closet: "O dad!"

The Old Man arose hurriedly and disappeared in the closet. Presently he reappeared. "His rheumatiz is coming on agin bad," he explained, "and he wants rubbin'." He lifted the demijohn of whiskey from the table and shook it.. It was empty. Dick Bullen put down his tin cup with an embarrassed laugh. So did the others. The Old Man examined their contents and said hopefully, "I reckon that's enough; he don't need much, You hold on all o' you for a spell, and I'll be back;" and vanished in the closet with an old flannel shirt and the whiskey. The door closed but imperfectly, and the following dialogue was distinctly audible:

"Now, sonny, whar does she ache worst?"

"Sometimes over yar and sometimes under yer; but it's most powerful from yer to yer. Rub yer, dad."

A silence seemed to indicate a brisk rubbing. Then Johnny

"Hevin' a good time out yer, dad?"

" Yes, sonny."

"To-morrer's Chrismiss,--ain't it?"

"Yes, sonny. How does she feel now?"

"Better. Rub a little furder down, Wot's Chrismiss, anyway? Wot's it all about?"

"Oh, it's a day."

This exhaustive definition was apparently satisfactory, for there was a silent interval of rubbing. Presently Johnny again:

"Mar sez that everywhere else but yer everybody gives things to everybody Chrismiss and then she jist waded inter you. She sez thar's a man they call Sandy Claws, not a white man, you know, but a kind o' Chinemin, comes down the chimbley night afore Chrismias and gives things to chillern,--boys like me. Puts 'em in their butes! Thet's what she tried to play upon me. Easy now, pop, whar are you rubbin' to,--thet's a mile from the place! She jest made that up, didn't she, jest to aggrewate me and you? Don't rub that. Why, dad!"

In the great quiet that seemed to have fallen upon the house the sigh of the near pines and the drip of leaves without was very distinct. Johnny's voice, too, was lowered as he went on, "Don't you take on now, for I'm gettin' all right fast. Wot's the boys doin' out thar?"

The Old Man partly opened the door and peered through. His guests were sitting there sociably enough, and there were a few silver coins and a lean buckskin purse on the table. "Bettin' on suthin'--some little game or 'nother. They're all right," he replied to Johnny, and recommenced his rubbing.

"I'd like to take a hand and win some money," said Johnny reflectively after a pause.

The Old Man glibly repeated what was evidently a familiar formula, that if Johnny would wait until he struck it rich in the tunnel he'd have lots of money, etc., etc.

"Yes," said Johnny, "but you don't. And whether you strike it or I win it, it's about the same. It's all luck. But it's mighty cur'o's about Chrismiss--ain't it? Why do they call it Chrismiss?"

Perhaps from some instinctive deference to the overhearing of his guests, or from. some vague sense of incongruity, the Old Man's reply was so low as to be inaudible beyond the room.

"Yes," said Johnny, with some slight abatement of interest, "I've heerd o' him before. thar, that'll do, dad. I don't ache near so bad as I did. Now wrap me tight in this yer blanket. So. Now," he added in a muffled whisper, "sit down yer by me till I go asleep." To assure himself of obedience, he disengaged one hand from the blanket, and, grasping his fatber's sleeve, again composed himself to rest.

For some moments the Old Man waited patiently. Then the unwonted stillness of the house excited his curiosity, and without moving from the bed he cautiously opened the door with his disengaged hand, and looked into the main room. To his infinite surprise it was dark and deserted. But even then a smouldering log on the hearth broke, and by the upspringing blaze he saw the figure of Dick Bullen sitting by the dying embers. "Hello!"

Dick started, rose, and came somewhat unsteadily toward him.

"Whar's the boys?" said the Old Man.

"Gone up the cañon on a little *pasear*. They coming back for me in a minit. I'm waitin' round for 'em. What are you starin' at, Old Man?" he added, with a forced laugh; "do you think I'm drunk?"

The Old Man might have been pardoned the supposition, for Dick's eyes were humid and his face flushed. He loitered and lounged back to the chimney, yawned, shook himself, buttoned up his coat and laughed. "Liquor ain't so plenty as that, Old Man. Now don't you git up," he continued, as the Old Man made a movement to release his sleeve from Johnny's hand, "Don't you mind manners. Sit jest whar you be; I'm goin' in a jiffy. Thar, that's them now."

There was a low tap at the door, Dick Bullen opened it quickly, nodded "Good-night" to his host, and disappeared. The Old Man would have followed him but for the hand that still unconsciously grasped his sleeve. He could have easily disengaged it: it was small, weak, and emaciated. But perhaps because it was small, weak, and emaciated he changed his mind, and, drawing his chair closer to the bed, rested his head upon it. In this defense-less attitude the potency of his earlier potations surprised him. The room flickered and faded before his eyes, reappeared, faded again, went out, and left him--asleep.

Meantime Dick Bullen, closing the door, confronted his companions. "Are you ready?" said Staples. "Ready," said Dick "what's the time?" "Past twelve," was the reply; "can you make it? it's nigh on fifty miles, the round trip hither and yon." "I reckon," returned Dick shortly. "What's the mare?" "Bill and Jack's holdin' her at the crossin'" "Let 'em hold on a minit longer," said Dick.

He turned and reentered the house softly. By the light of the guttering candle and dying fire he saw that the door of the little room was open. He stepped toward it on tip-toe and looked in. The Old Man had fallen back in his chair, snoring, his helpless feet thrust out in a line with his collapsed shoulders, and his hat pulled over his eyes. Beside him, on a narrow wooden bedstead, lay Johnny, muffled tightly in a blanket that hid all save a strip of forehead and a few curls damp with perspiration. Dick Bullen made a step forward, hesitated, and glanced over his shoulder into the deserted room. Everything was quiet. With a sudden resolution he parted his huge mustache, with both hands and stooped over the sleeping boy. But even as he did so a mischievous blast, lying in wait, swooped down the chimney, rekindled the hearth, and lit up the room with a shameless glow from which Dick fled in bashful terror.

His companions were already waiting for him at the crossing. Two of them were struggling in the darkness with some strange misshapen bulk, which an Dick came nearer took the semblance of a great yellow horse.

178

It was the mare. She wan not a pretty picture. From her Roman nose to her rising haunches, from her arched spine hidden by the stiff machillas of a Mexican saddle, to her thick, straight bony legs, there was not a line of equine grace. In her half-blind but wholly vicious white eyes, in her protruding under-lip, in her monstrous color, there was nothing but ugliness and vice.

"Niow then," said Staples, "stand cl'ar of her heels, boys, and up with you. Don't miss your first holt of her mane, and mind ye get your off stirrup quick. Ready!"

There was a leap, a scrambling struggle, a bound, a wild retreat of the crowd, a circle of flying hoofs, two springless leaps that jarred the earth, a rapid play and jingle of spurs, a plunge, and then the voice of Dick somewhere in the darkness. "All right!"

"Don't take the lower road back onless you're hard pushed for time! Don't hold her in downhill! We'll be at the ford at five. G'lang! Hoopa! Mula! GO!"

A splash, a spark struck from the ledge in the road, a clatter in the rocky cut beyond, and Dick was gone.

Sing, O Muse, the ride of Richard Bullen! Sing, O Muse, of chivalrous men! the sacred quest, the doughty deeds, the battery of low churls, the fearsome ride and gruesome perils of the Flower of Simpson's Bar! Alack! she is dainty, this Muse! She will have none of this bucking brute and swaggering, ragged rider, and I must fain follow him in prose, afoot!

It was one o'clock, and yet he had only gained Rattle-snake Hill. For in that time Jovita had rehearsed to him all her imperfections and practiced all her vices. Thrice had she stumbled. Twice had she thrown up her Roman nose in a straight line with the reins, and resisting bit and spur, struck out madly across country. Twice had she reared,

179

and rearing, fallen backward; and twice had the agile Dick, unharmed, regained his seat before she found her vicious legs again. And a mile beyond them, at the foot of a long hill, was Rattlesnake Creek. Dick knew that here was the crucial test of his ability to perform his enterprise, set his teeth grimly, put his knees well into her flanks, and changed his defensive tactics to brisk aggression. Bullied and maddened, Jovita began the descent of the hill. Here the artful Richard pretended to hold her in with ostentatious objurgation and well-feigned cries of alarm. It is unnecessary to add that Jovita instantly ran away. Nor need I state the time made in the descent; it is written in the chronicles of Simpson's Bar. Enough that in another moment, as it seemed to Dick, she was splashing on the overflowed banks of Rattlesnake Creek. As Dick expected, the momentum she had acquired carried her beyond the point of balking, and holding her well together for a mighty leap, they dashed into the middle of the swiftly flowing current. A few moments of kicking, wading, and swimming, and Dick drew a long breath on the opposite bank.

The road from Rattlesnake Creek to Red Mountain was tolerably level. Either the plunge in Rattlesnake Creek had dampened her baleful fire, or the art which led to it had shown her the superior wickedness ot her rider, for Jovita no longer wasted her surplus energy in wanton conceits. Once she bucked, but it was from force of habit; once she shied, but it was from a new, freshly painted meeting-house at the crossing of the county road. Hollows, ditches, gravelly deposits, patches of freshly springing grasses, flew from beneath her rattling hoofs. She began to smell unpleasantly, once or twice she coughed slightly, but there was no abatement of her strength or speed. By two o'clock he had passed Red Mountain and begun the descent to the plain. Ten minutes later the driver of the fast Pioneer coach was overtaken and passed by a "man on a pinto hoss"--an event sufficiently notable for remark. At half-past two Dick rose in his stirrups with a great shout. Stars were glittering through the rifted clouds, and beyond him, out of the plain, rose two spires, a flagstaff, and a strag-gling line of black objects. Dick jingled his spurs and swung his *riata*, Jovita bounded forward, and in another moment they swept into Tuttleville, and drew up before the wooden piazza of "The Hotel of All Nations."

What transpired that night at Tuttleville is not strictly a part of this record. Briefly I may state, however, that after Jovita had been handed over to a sleepy ostler, whom she at once kicked into unpleasant consciousness, Dick sallied out with the barkeeper for a tour of the sleeping town. Lights still gleamed from a few saloons and gambling houses; but avoiding these, they stopped before several closed shops, and by persistent tapping and judicious out-cry roused the proprietors from their beds, and made them unbar the doors of their magazines and expose their wares. Sometimes they were met by curses, but oftener by interest and some concern in their needs, and the inter-view was invariably concluded by a drink. It was three o'clock before this pleasantry was given over, and with a small waterproof bag of India rubber strapped on his shoulders, Dick returned to the hotel. But here he was waylaid by Beauty--Beauty opulent in charms, affluent in dress, persuasive in speech, and Spanish in accent! In vain she repeated the invitation in "Excelsior," happily scorned by all Alpine-climbing youth, and rejected by this child of the Sierras--a rejection softened in this instance by a laugh and his last gold coin. And then he sprang to the saddle

and dashed down the lonely street and out into the lone-
lier plain, where presently the lights, the black line of
houses, the spires, and the flagstaff sank into the earth behind him again and were lost in the distance.

The storm had cleared away, the air was brisk and cold,
the outlines of adjacent landmarks were distinct, but it was
half-past four before Dick reached the meetinghouse and
the crossing of the county road. To avoid the rising grade
he had taken a longer and more circuitous road, in whose
viscid mud Jovita sank fetlock deep at every bound. It was
a poor preparation for a steady ascent of five miles more;
but Jovita, gathering her legs under her, took it with her
usual blind, unreasoning fury, and a half-hour later
reached the long level that led to Rattlesnake Creek. Another half-hour would bring him to the creek. He threw
the reins lightly upon the neck of the mare, chirruped to
her, and began to sing.

Suddenly Jovita shied with a bound that would have
unseated a less practiced rider. Hanging to her rein was a
figure that had leaped from the bank, and at the same time
from the road before her arose a shadowy horse and rider.

"Throw up your hands," commanded the second appa-
rition, with an oath.

Dick felt the mare tremble, quiver, and apparently sink
under him. He knew what it meant and was prepared.
"Stand aside, Jack Simpson. I know you, you d----d thief!
Let me pass, or-- He did not finish the sentence. Jovita rose
straight in the air with a terrific bound, throwing the figure from her bit with a single shake of her vicious head,
and charged with deadly malevolence down on the im-
pediment before her. An oath, a pistol shot, horse and
highwayman rolled over in the road, and the next moment
Jovita was a hundred yards away. But the good right arm

of her rider, shattered by a bullet, dropped helplessly at his side.

Without slacking his speed he shifted the reins to his left hand. But a few moments later he was obliged to halt and tighten the saddle girths that had slipped in the onset. This in his crippled condition took some time. He had no fear of pursuit, but looking up he saw that the eastern stars were already paling, and that the distant peaks had lost their ghostly whiteness and now stood out blackly against a lighter sky. Day was upon him. Then completely ab-sorbed in a single idea, he forgot the pain of his wound, and mounting again dashed on toward Rattlesnake Creek. But now Jovita's breath came broken by gasps, Dick reeled in his saddle, and brighter and brighter grew the sky.

Ride, Richard; run, Jovita; linger, O day!

For the last few rods there was a roaring in his ears. Was it exhaustion from loss of blood, or what? He was dazed and giddy as he swept down the hill, and did not recognize his surroundings. Had he taken the wrong road, or was this Rattlesnake Creek?

It was. But the brawling creek he had swum a few hours before had risen, more than doubled its volume, and now rolled a swift and resistless river between him and Rattle-snake Hill. For the first time that night Richard's heart sank within him. The river, the mountain, the quickening east, swam before his eyes. He shut them to recover his self-control. In that brief interval, by some fantastic mental process, the little room at Simpson's Bar and the figures of the sleeping father and son rose upon him. He opened his eyes wildly, cast off his coat, pistol, boots, and saddle, bound his precious pack tightly to his shoulders, grasped the bare flanks of Jovita with his bared knees, and with a shout dashed into the yellow water. A cry rose from the opposite bank as the head of a man and horse struggled for a few moments against the battling current, and then were swept away amidst uprooted trees and whirling driftwood.

The Old Man started and woke. The fire on the hearth was dead, the candle in the outer room flickering in its socket, and somebody was rapping at the door. He opened it, but fell back with a cry before the dripping, half-naked figure that reeled against the doorpost.

"Dick?"

"Hush! Is he awake yet?"

"No; but, Dick--"

"Dry up, you old fool! Get me some whiskey, quick!" The Old Man flew and returned with--an empty bottle! Dick would have sworn, but his strength was not equal to the occasion. He staggered, caught at the handle of the door, and motioned to the Old Man.

"Thar's suthin' in my pack yet for Johnny. Take it off. I can't."

The Old Man unstrapped the pack, and laid it before the exhausted man.

"Open it, quick."

He did so with trembling fingers. It contained only a few poor toys--cheap and barbaric enough, goodness knows, but bright with paint and tinsel. One of them was broken; another, I fear, was irretrievably ruined by water, and on the third--ah me! there was a cruel spot.

"It don't look like much, that's a fact," said Dick rue-fully. . . . "But it's the best we could do . . . Take 'em, Old Man, and put `em in his stocking, and tell him--tell him, you know--hold me, Old Man--" The Old Man caught at his sinking figure. "Tell him," said Dick, with a weak little laugh--"tell him Sandy Claus has come."

And even so, bedraggled, ragged, unshaven and un-shorn, with one arm hanging helplessly at his side, Santa Claus came to Simpson's Bar and fell fainting on the first threshold. The Christmas dawn came slowly after, touching the remoter peaks with the rosy warmth of ineffable love. And it looked so tenderly on Simpson's Bar that the whole mountain, as if caught in a generous action, blushed to the skies.

XIII The Snow Man

By O. Henry and Harris Merton Lyon

HOUSED and windowpaned from it, the greatest wonder to little children is the snow. To men, it is something like a crucible in which their world melts into a white star ten million miles away. The man who can stand the test is a Snow Man; and this is his reading by Fahrenheit, Réaumur, or Moses's carven tablets of stone.

Night had fluttered a sable pinion above the cañon of Big Lost River, and I urged my horse toward the Bay Horse Ranch because the snow was deepening. The flakes were as large as an hour's circular tatting by Miss Wilkins's ablest spinster, betokening a heavy snowfall and less entertainment and more adventure than the completion of the tatting could promise. I knew Ross Curtis of the Bay Horse, and that I would be welcome as a snow-bound pilgrim, both for hospitality's sake and because Ross had few chances to confide in living creatures who did not neigh, bellow, bleat, yelp, or howl during his discourse.

The ranch house was just within the jaws of the cañon where its builder may have fatuously fancied that the timbered and rocky walls on both sides would have protected it from the wintry Colorado winds; but I feared the drift. Even now through the endless, bottomless rift in the hills--the speaking tube of the four winds--came roaring the voice of the proprietor to the little room on the top floor.

At my "hello," a ranch hand came from an outer building and received my thankful horse. In another minute, Ross and I sat by a stove in the dining-room of the four-room ranch house, while the big, simple welcome of the household lay at my disposal. Fanned by the whizzing norther, the fine, dry snow was sifted and bolted through the cracks and knotholes of the logs. The cook room, without separating door, appended.

In there I could see a short, sturdy, leisurely and weather-beaten man moving with professional sureness about his red-hot stove. His face was stolid and unreadable--something like that of a great thinker, or of one who had no thoughts to conceal. I thought his eye seemed unwarrantably superior to the elements and to the man, but quickly attributed that to the characteristic self-importance of a petty chef. "Camp cook" was the niche that I gave him in the Hall of Types; and he fitted it as an apple fits a dumpling.

Cold it was in spite of the glowing stove; and Ross and I sat and talked, shuddering frequently, half from nerves and half from the freezing draughts. So he brought the bottle and the cook brought boiling water, and we made prodigious hot toddies against the attacks of Boreas. We clinked glasses often. They sounded like icicles dropping from the eaves, or like the tinkle of a thousand prisms of a Louis XIV chandelier that I once heard at a boarders' dance in the parlor of a ten-a-week boarding-house in Gramercy Square. Sic transit.

Silence in the terrible beauty of the snow and of the Sphinx and of the stars; but they who believe that all things, from a without-wine table d'hôte to the crucifixion, may be interpreted through music, might have found a nocturne or a symphony to express the isolation of that blotted-out world. The clink of glass and bottle, the æolian chorus of the wind in the house crannies, its deeper trombone through the cañon below, and the Wagnerian crash of the cook's pots and pans, united in a fit, discordant melody, I thought. No less welcome an accompaniment was the sizzling of broiling ham and venison cutlets, indorsed by the solvent fumes of true Java, bringing rich promises of comfort to our yearning souls.

The cook brought the smoking supper to the table. He nodded to me democratically as he cast the heavy plates around as though he were pitching quoits or hurling the discus. I looked at him with some appraisement and curiosity and much conciliation. There was no prophet to tell us when that drifting evil outside might cease to fall; and it is well, when snow-bound, to stand somewhere within the radius of the cook's favorable consideration. But I could read neither favor nor disapproval in the face and manner of our pot-wrestler.

He was about five feet nine inches, and two hundred pounds of commonplace, bull-necked, pink-faced, callous calm. He wore brown duck trousers too tight and too short, and a blue flannel shirt with sleeves rolled above his elbows. There was a sort of grim, steady scowl on his features that looked to me as though he had fixed it there purposely as a protection against the weakness of an inherent amiability that, he fancied, were better concealed. And then I let supper usurp his brief occupancy of my thoughts.

"Draw up, George," said Ross. "Let's all eat while the grub's hot."

"You fellows go on and chew," answered the cook. "I ate mine in the kitchen before sun-down."

"Think it'll be a big snow, George?" asked the ranchman.

George had turned to reënter the cook room. He moved slowly around and, looking at his face, it seemed to me that he was turning over the wisdom and knowledge of centuries in his head.

"It might," was his delayed reply.

At the door of the kitchen he stopped and looked back at us. Both Ross and I held our knives and forks poised and gave him our regard. Some men have the power of drawing the attention of others without speaking a word. Their attitude is more effective than a shout.

"And again it mightn't," said George, and went back to his stove.

After we had eaten, he came in and gathered the emptied dishes. He stood for a moment, while his spurious frown deepened.

"It might stop any minute," he said, "or it might keep up for days."

At the farther end of the cook room I saw George pour hot water into his dishpan, light his pipe, and put the tableware through its required lavation. He then carefully unwrapped from a piece of old saddle blanket a paperback book, and settled himself to read by his dim oil lamp.

And then the ranchman threw tobacco on the cleared table and set forth again the bottles and glasses; and I saw that I stood in a deep channel through which the long dammed flood of his discourse would soon be booming. But I was half content, comparing my fate with that of the late Thomas Tucker, who had to sing for his supper, thus doubling the burdens of both himself and his host.

"Snow is a hell of a thing," said Ross, by way of a foreword. "It ain't, somehow, it seems to me, salubrious. I can stand water and mud and two inches below zero and a hundred and ten in the shade and medium-sized cyclones, but this here fuzzy white stuff naturally gets me all locoed. I reckon the reason it rattles you is because it changes the look of things so much. It's like you had a wife and left her in the morning with the same old blue cotton wrapper on, and rides in of a night and runs across her all outfitted in a white silk evening frock, waving an ostrich-feather fan, and monkeying with a posy of lily flowers. Wouldn't it make you look for your pocket compass? You'd be liable to kiss her before you collected your presence of mind."

By and by, the flood of Ross's talk was drawn up into the clouds (so it pleased me to fancy) and there condensed into the finer snowflakes of thought; and we sat silent about the stove, as good friends and bitter enemies will do. I thought of Ross's preamble about the mysterious influence upon man exerted by that ermine-lined monster that now covered our little world, and knew he was right.

Of all the curious knickknacks, mysteries, puzzles, Indian gifts, rat-traps, and well-disguised blessings that the gods chuck down to us from the Olympian peaks, the most disquieting and evil-bringing is the snow. By scientific analysis it is absolute beauty and purity--so, at the beginning we look doubtfully at chemistry.

It falls upon the world, and lo! we live in another. It hides in a night the old scars and familiar places with which we have grown heart-sick or enamored. So, as quietly as we can, we hustle on our embroidered robes and hie us on Prince Camaralzaman's horse or in the reindeer sleigh into the white country where the seven colors converge. This is when our fancy can overcome the bane of it.

But in certain spots of the earth comes the snow-madness, made known by people turned wild and distracted by the bewildering veil that has obscured the only world they know. In the cities, the white fairy who sets the brains of her dupes whirling by a wave of her wand is cast for the comedy rôle. Her diamond shoe buckles glitter like frost; with a pirouette she invites the spotless carnival.

But in the waste places the snow is sardonic. Sponging out the world of the outliers, it gives no foothold on another sphere in return. It makes of the earth a firmament under foot; it leaves us clawing and stumbling in space in an inimical fifth element whose evil outdoes its strangeness and beauty. There Nature, low comedienne, plays her tricks on man. Though she has put him forth as her highest product, it appears that she has fashioned him with what seems almost incredible carelessness and indexterity. One-sided and without balance, with his two halves unequally fashioned and joined, must he ever jog his eccentric way. The snow falls, the darkness caps it, and the ridiculous man-biped strays in accurate circles until he succumbs in the ruins of his defective architecture.

In the throat of the thirsty the snow is vitriol. In appearance as plausible as the breakfast food of the angels, it is as hot in the mouth as ginger, increasing the pangs of the water-famished. It is a derivative from water, air, and some cold, uncanny fire from which the caloric has been extracted. Good has been said of it; even the poets, crazed by its spell and shivering in their attics under its touch, have indited permanent melodies commemorative of its beauty.

Still, to the saddest overcoated optimist it is a plague--a corroding plague that Pharaoh successfully side-stepped. It beneficently covers the wheat fields, swelling the crop-- and the Flour Trust gets us by the throat like a sudden quinsy. It spreads the tail of its white kirtle over the red seams of the rugged north--and the Alaska short story is born. Etiolated perfidy, it shelters the mountain traveler burrowing from the icy air--and, melting to-morrow, drowns his brother in the valley below.

At its worst it is lock and key and crucible, and the wand of Circe. When it corrals man in lonely ranches, mountain cabins, and forest huts, the snow makes apes and tigers of the hardiest. It turns the bosoms of weaker ones to glass, their tongues to infants' rattles, their hearts to lawlessness and spleen. It is not all from the isolation; the snow is not merely a blockader; it is a Chemical Test. It is a good man who can show a reaction that is not chiefly composed of a drachm or two of potash and magnesia, with traces of Adam, Ananias, Nebuchadnezzar, and the fretful porcupine.

This is no story, you say; well, let it begin.

There was a knock at the door (is the opening not full of context and reminiscence oh, best buyers of best sellers?).

We drew the latch, and in stumbled Étienne Girod (as he afterward named himself). But just then he was no more than a worm struggling for life, enveloped in a killing white chrysalis.

We dug down through snow, overcoats, mufflers, and waterproofs, and dragged forth a living thing with a Van Dyck beard and marvelous diamond rings. We put it through the approved curriculum of snow-rubbing, hot milk, and teaspoonful doses of whiskey, working him up to a graduating class entitled to a diploma of three fingers of rye in half a glassful of hot water. One of the ranch boys had already come from the quarters at Ross's bugle-like yell and kicked the stranger's staggering pony to some sheltered corral where beasts were entertained.

Let a paragraphic biography of Girod intervene.

Étienne was an opera singer originally, we gathered; but adversity and the snow had made him *non compos vocis*. The adversity consisted of the stranded San Salvador Opera Company, a period of hotel second-story work, and then a career as a professional palmist, jumping from town to town.

For, like other professional palmists, every time he worked the Heart Line too strongly he immediately moved along the Line of Least Resistance. Though Étienne did not confide this to us, we surmised that he had moved out into the dusk about twenty minutes ahead of a constable, and had thus encountered the snow. In his most sacred blue language he dilated upon the subject of snow; for Étienne was Paris-born and loved the snow with the same passion that an orchid does.

"Mee-ser-rhable!" commented Étienne and took another three fingers. "Complete, cast-iron, pussy-footed, blank . . . blank!" said Ross, and followed suit.

"Rotten," said I.

The cook said nothing. He stood in the door weighing our outburst; and insistently from behind that frozen visage I got two messages (via the M. A. M. wireless). One was that George considered our vituperation against the snow childish; the other was that George did not love Dagoes. Inasmuch as Étienne was a Frenchman, I concluded I had the message wrong. So I queried the other: "Bright eyes, you don't really mean Dagoes, do you?" and over the wireless came three deathly, psychic taps: "Yes." Then I reflected that to George all foreigners were probably "Dagoes." I had once known another camp cook who had thought Mons., Sig., and Millie (Trans-Mississippi for Mlle.) were Italian given names; this cook used to marvel therefore at the paucity of Neo-Roman precognomens, and therefore why not--

I have said that snow is a test of men. For one day, two days, Étienne stood at the window, Fletcherizing his finger nails and shrieking and moaning at the monotony. To me, Étienne was just about as unbearable as the snow; and so, seeking relief, I went out on the second day to look at my horse, slipped on a stone, broke my collarbone, and thereafter underwent not the snow test, but the test of flat-on-the-back. A test that comes once too often for any man to stand.

However, I bore up cheerfully. I was now merely a spectator, and from my couch in the big room I could lie and watch the human interplay with that detached, impassive, impersonal feeling which French writers tell us is so valuable to the littéateur, and American writers to the faro-dealer.

"I shall go crazy in this abominable, mee-ser-rhable place!" was Étienne's constant prediction.

"Never knew Mark Twain to bore me before," said Ross, over and over. He sat by the other window, hour after hour, a box of Pittsburgh stogies of the length, strength, and odor of a Pittsburgh graft scandal deposited on one side of him, and "Roughing It," "The Jumping Frog," and "Life on the Mississippi" on the other. For every chapter he lit a new stogy, puffing furiously. This, in time, gave him a recurrent premonition of cramps, gastritis, smoker's colic, or whatever it is they have in Pittsburg after a too deep indulgence in graft scandals. To fend off the colic, Ross resorted time and again to Old Doctor Still's Amber-Colored U. S. A. Colic Cure. Result, after forty-eight hours--nerves.

"Positive fact I never knew Mark Twain to make me tired before. Positive fact." Ross slammed "Roughing It" on the floor. "When you're snowbound this-away you want tragedy, I guess. Humor just seems to bring out all your cussedness. You read a man's poor, pitiful attempts to be funny and it makes you so nervous you want to tear the book up, get out your bandana, and have a good, long cry."

At the other end of the room, the Frenchman took his finger nails out of his mouth long enough to exclaim:

"Humor! Humor at such a time as thees! My God, I shall go crazy in thees abominable--"

"Supper," announced George.

These meals were not the meals of Rabelais who said, "the great God makes the planets and we make the platters neat." By that time, the ranch-house meals were not affairs of gusto; they were mental distraction, not bodily proven-der. What they were to be later shall never be forgotten by Ross or me or Étienne.

After supper, the stogies and finger nails began again. My shoulder ached wretchedly, and with half-closed eyes I tried to forget it by watching the deft movements of the stolid cook.

Suddenly I saw him cock his ear, like a dog. Then, with a swift step, he moved to the door, threw it open, and stood there.

The rest of us had heard nothing.

"What is it, George ?" asked Ross.

The cook reached out his hand into the darkness along-side the jamb. With careful precision he prodded something. Then he made one careful step into the snow. His back muscles bulged a little under the arms as he stooped and lightly lifted a burden. Another step inside the door, which he shut methodically behind him, and he dumped the burden at a safe distance from the fire.

He stood up and fixed us with a solemn eye. None of us moved under that Orphic suspense until,

"A woman," remarked George.

Miss Willie Adams was her name. Vocation, school-teacher. Present avocation, getting lost in the snow. Age, yum-yum (the Persian for twenty). Take to the woods if you would describe Miss Adams. A willow for grace; a hickory for fibre; a birch for the clear whiteness of her skin; her eyes, the blue sky seen through treetops; the silk in cocoons for her hair; her voice, the murmur of the evening June wind in the leaves; her mouth, the berries of the wintergreen; fingers as light as ferns; her toe as small as a deer track. General impression upon the dazed beholder--you could not see the forest for the trees.

Psychology, with a capital P and the foot of a lynx, at this juncture stalks into the ranch house. Three men, a cook, a pretty young woman--all snowbound. Count me out of it, as I did not count, anyway. I never did, with women. Count the cook out, if you like. But note the effect upon Ross and Étienne Girod.

Ross dumped Mark Twain in a trunk and locked the trunk. Also, he discarded the Pittsburgh scandals. Also, he shaved off a three days' beard.

Étienne, being French, began on the beard first. He pomaded it, from a little tube of grease Hongroise in his vest pocket. He combed it with a little aluminum comb from the same vest pocket. He trimmed it with manicure scissors from the same vest pocket. His light and Gallic spirits underwent a sudden, miraculous change. He hummed a blithe San Salvador Opera Company tune; he grinned, smirked, bowed, pirouetted, twiddled, twaddled, twisted, and tooralooed. Gayly, the notorious troubadour could not have equalled Étienne.

Ross's method of advance was brusque, domineering. "Little woman," he said, "you're welcome here!"--and with what he thought subtle double meaning--"welcome to stay here as long as you like, snow or no snow."

Miss Adams thanked him a little wildly, some of the wintergreen berries creeping into the birch bark. She looked around hurriedly as if seeking escape. But there was none, save the kitchen and the room allotted her. She made an excuse and disappeared into her own room. Later I, feigning sleep, heard the following:

"Mees Adams, I was almos' to perish-die-of-monotony w'en your fair and beautiful face appear in thees mee-ser-rhable house." I opened my starboard eye. The beard was being curled furiously around a finger, the Svengali eye was rolling, the chair was being hunched closer to the school-teacher's. "I am French--you see--temperamental--nervous! I cannot endure thees dull hours in thees ranch house; but--a woman comes! Ah!" The shoulders gave nine 'rahs and a tiger. "What a difference! All is light and gay; ever'ting smile w'en you smile. You have 'eart, beauty, grace. My 'cart comes back to me w'en I feel your 'eart. So!" He laid his hand upon his vest pocket. From this vantage point he suddenly snatched at the school-teacher's own hand. "Ah! Mees Adams, if I could only tell you how I ad--"

"Dinner," remarked George. He was standing just behind the Frenchman's ear. His eyes looked straight into the school-teacher's eyes. After thirty seconds of survey, his lips moved, deep in the flinty, frozen maelstrom of his face: "Dinner," he concluded, "will be ready in two minutes."

Miss Adams jumped to her feet, relieved. "I must get ready for dinner," she said brightly, and went into her room.

Ross came in fifteen minutes late. After the dishes had been cleaned away, I waited until a propitious time when the room was temporarily ours alone, and told him what had happened.

He became so excited that he lit a stogy without thinking. "Yeller-hided, unwashed, palm-readin' skunk," he said under his breath. "I'll shoot him full o' holes if he don't watch out--talkin' that way to my wife!"

I gave a jump that set my collarbone back another week. "Your wife!" I gasped.

"Well, I mean to make her that," he announced.

The air in the ranch house the rest of that day was tense with pent-up emotions, oh, best buyers of best sellers.

Ross watched Miss Adams as a hawk does a hen; he watched Étienne as a hawk does a scarecrow. Étienne watched Miss Adams as a weasel does a henhouse. He paid no attention to Ross.

The condition of Miss Adams, in the rôle of sought-after, was feverish. Lately escaped from the agony and long torture of the white cold, where for hours Nature had kept the little school-teacher's vision locked in and turned upon herself, nobody knows through what profound feminine introspections she had gone. Now, suddenly cast among men, instead of finding relief and security, she beheld herself plunged anew into other discomforts. Even in her own room she could hear the loud voices of her imposed suitors. "I'll blow you full o' holes!" shouted Ross. "Witnesses," shrieked Étienne, waving his hand at the cook and me. She could not have known the previous harassed condition of the men, fretting under indoor conditions. All she knew was, that where she had expected the frank freemasonry of the West, she found the subtle tangle of two men's minds, bent upon exacting whatever romance there might be in her situation.

She tried to dodge Ross and the Frenchman by spells of nursing me. They also came over to help nurse. This combination aroused such a natural state of invalid cussedness on my part that they were all forced to retire. Once she did manage to whisper: "I am so worried here. I don't know what to do."

what to do."

To which I replied, gently, hitching up my shoulder, that I was a hunch-savant and that the Eighth House under this sign, the Moon being in Virgo, showed that everything would turn out all right.

But twenty minutes later I saw Étienne reading her palm and felt that perhaps I might have to recast her horoscope, and try for a dark man coming with a bundle.

Toward sunset, Étienne left the house for a few moments and Ross, who had been sitting taciturn and morose, having unlocked Mark Twain, made another dash. It was typical Ross talk.

He stood in front of her and looked down majestically at that cool and perfect spot where Miss Adams' forehead met the neat part in her fragrant hair. First, however, he cast a desperate glance at me. I was in a profound slumber.

"Little woman," he began, "it's certainly tough for a man like me to see you bothered this way. You"--gulp--"you have been alone in this world too long. You need a protector. I might say that at a time like this you need a protector the worst kind--a protector who would take a three-ring delight in smashing the saffron-colored kisser off of any yeller-skinned skunk that made himself obnoxious to you. Hem. Hem. I am a lonely man, Miss Adams. I have so far had to carry on my life without the"--gulp--"sweet radiance"--gulp--"of a woman around the house. I feel especially doggoned lonely at a time like this, when I am pretty near locoed from havin' to stall indoors, and hence it was with delight I welcomed your first appearance in this here shack.

Since then I have been packed jam full of more different kinds of feelings, ornery, mean, dizzy, and superb, than has fallen my way in years." Miss Adams made a useless movement toward escape. The Ross chin stuck firm. "I don't want to annoy you, Miss Adams, but, by heck, if it comes to that you'll have to be annoyed. And I'll have to have my say. This palm-ticklin' slob of a Frenchman ought to be kicked off the place and if you'll say the word, off he goes. But I don't want to do the wrong thing. You've got to show a preference. I'm gettin' around to the point, Miss-- Miss Willie, in my own brick fashion. I've stood about all I can stand these last two days and somethin's got to happen. The suspense hereabouts is enough to hang a sheepherder. Miss Willie"--he lassooed her hand by main force--"just say the word. You need somebody to take your part all your life long. Will you mar--" "Supper," remarked George, tersely, from the kitchen door, Miss Adams hurried away. Ross turned angrily. "You--" "I have been revolving it in my head," said George.

He brought the coffee pot forward heavily. Then bravely the big platter of pork and beans. Then somberly the potatoes. Then profoundly the biscuits. "I have been revolving it in my mind. There ain't no use waitin' any longer for Swengalley. Might as well eat now."

From my excellent vantage-point on the couch I watched the progress of that meal. Ross, muddled, glowering, disappointed; Étienne, eternally blandishing, attentive, ogling; Miss Adams, nervous, picking at her food, hesitant about answering questions, almost hysterical; now and then the solid, flitting shadow of the cook, passing behind their backs like a Dreadnaught in a fog.

I used to own a clock which gurgled in its throat three minutes before it struck the hour. I know, therefore, the slow freight of Anticipation. For I have awakened at three in the morning, heard the clock gurgle, and waited those three minutes for the three strokes I knew were to come. *Alors.* In Ross's ranch house that night the slow freight of Climax whistled in the distance.

Étienne began it after supper. Miss Adams had suddenly displayed a lively interest in the kitchen layout and I could see her in there, chatting brightly at George--not with him--the while he ducked his head and rattled his pans.

"My fren'," said Étienne, exhaling a large cloud from his cigarette and patting Ross lightly on the shoulder with a bediamonded hand which hung limp from a yard or more of bony arm, "I see I mus' be frank with you. Firs', because we are rivals; second, because you take these matters so serious. I--I am Frenchman. I love the women"--he threw back his curls, bared his yellow teeth, and blew an unsavory kiss toward the kitchen. "It is, I suppose, a trait of my nation. All Frenchmen love the women--pretty women.

Now, look: Here I am!" He spread out his arms. "Cold outside! I detes' the col--l--l'! Snow! I abominate the messer-rhable snow! Two men! This"--pointing to me--"an' this!" Pointing to Ross. "I am distracted! For two whole days I stan' at the window an' tear my 'air! I am nervous, upset, pr-r-ro-foun'ly distress inside my 'cad! An' suddenly--be'old! A woman, a nice, pretty, charming, innocen' young woman! I, naturally, rejoice. I become myself again--gay, light-'earted, 'appy. I address myself to mademoiselle; it passes the time. That, m'sieu', is wot the women are for--pass the time! Entertainment--like the music, like the wine!

"They appeal to the mood, the caprice, the temperamen'. To play with thees woman, follow her through her humor, pursue her--ah! that is the mos' delightful way to sen' the hours about their business."

Ross banged the table. "Shut up, you miserable yeller

201

pup!" he roared. "I object to your pursuin' anything or anybody in my house. Now, you listen to me, you--" He
picked up the box of stogies and used it on the table as an
emphasizer. The noise of it awoke the attention of the girl
in the kitchen. Unheeded, she crept into the room. "I don't
know anything about your French ways of lovemakin' an'
I don't care. In my section of the country, it's the best man
wins. And I'm the best man here, and don't you forget it!
This girl's goin' to be mine.

There ain't going to be any playing, or philandering, or
palm reading about it. I've made up my mind I'll have this
girl, and that settles it. My word is the law in this neck o'
the woods. She's mine, and as soon as she says she's mine,
you pull out." The box made one final, tremendous punc-
tuation point.

Étienne's bravado was unruffled. "Ah! that is no way to
win a woman," he smiled, easily. "I make prophecy you
will never win 'er that way. No. Not thees woman. She
mus' be played along an' then keessed, this charming, deli-
cious little creature. One kees! An' then you 'ave her."
Again he displayed his unpleasant teeth. "I make you a bet
I will kees her--"

As a cheerful chronicler of deeds done well, it joys me
to relate that the hand which fell upon Étienne's amorous
lips was not his own. There was one sudden sound, as of a
mule kicking a lath fence, and then--through the swinging
doors of oblivion for Étienne.

I had seen this blow delivered. It was an aloof, unstud-
ied, almost absent-minded affair. I had thought the cook
was rehearsing the proper method of turning a flapjack.

Silently, lost in thought, he stood there scratching his
head. Then he began rolling down his sleeves.

"You'd better get your things on, Miss, and we'll get out

of here," he decided. "Wrap up warm."

I heard her heave a little sigh of relief as she went to get her cloak, sweater, and hat.

Ross jumped to his feet, and said: "George, what are you goin' to do?" George, who had been headed in my direction, slowly swivelled around and faced his employer. "Bein' a camp cook, I ain't over-burdened with hosses," George enlightened us. "Therefore, I am going to try to borrow this feller's here."

For the first time in four days my soul gave a genuine cheer. "If it's for Lochinvar purposes, go as far as you like," I said, grandly.

The cook studied me a moment, as if trying to find an insult in my words. "No," he replied. "It's for mine and the young lady's purposes, and we'll go only three miles--to Hicksville. Now let me tell you somethin', Ross." Suddenly I was confronted with the cook's chunky back and I heard a low, curt, carrying voice shoot through the room at my host. George had wheeled just as Ross started to speak. "You're, nutty. That's what's the matter with you. You can't stand the snow. You're gettin' nervouser, and nuttier every day. That and this Dago"--he jerked a thumb at the half-dead Frenchman in the corner--"has got you to the point where I thought I better horn in. I got to revolvin' it around in my mind and I seen if somethin' wasn't done, and done soon, there'd be murder around here and maybe"--his head gave an imperceptible list toward the girl's room--"worse."

He stopped, but he held up a stubby finger to keep any one else from speaking. Then he plowed slowly through the drift of his ideas. "About this here woman. I know you, Ross, and I know what you reely think about women. If she hadn't happened in here durin' this here snow, you'd never have given two thoughts to the whole woman question. Likewise, when the storm clears, and you and the boys go hustlin' out, this here whole business'll clear out of your head and you won't think of a skirt again until Kingdom Come. Just because o' this snow here, don't forget you're livin' in the selfsame world you was in four days ago. And you're the same man, too. Now, what's the use o' gettin' all snarled up over four days of stickin' in the house? That there's what I been revolvin' in my mind and this here's the decision I've come to."

He plodded to the door and shouted to one of the ranch hands to saddle my horse.

Ross lit a stogy and stood thoughtful in the middle of the room. Then he began: "I've a durn good notion, George, to knock your confounded head off and throw you into that snowbank, if--"

"You're wrong, mister. That ain't a durned good notion you've got. It's durned bad. Look here!" He pointed steadily out of doors until we were both forced to follow his finger. "You're in here for more'n a week yet." After allowing this fact to sink in, he barked out at Ross: "Can you cook ?" Then at me: "Can you cook?" Then he looked at the wreck of Étienne and sniffed.

There was an embarrassing silence as Ross and I thought solemnly of a foodless week.

"If you just use hoss sense," concluded George, "and don't go for to hurt my feelin's, all I want to do is to take this young gal down to Hicksvile; and then I'll head back here and cook fer you."

The horse and Miss Adams arrived simultaneously, both of them very serious and quiet. The horse because he knew what he had before him in that weather; the girl because of what she had left behind.

Then all at once I awoke to a realization of what the cook was doing. "My God, man!" I cried, "aren't you afraid to go out in that snow?"

Behind my back I heard Ross mutter, "Not him."

George lifted the girl daintily up behind the saddle, drew on his gloves, put his foot in the stirrup, and turned to inspect me leisurely.

As I passed slowly in his review, I saw in my mind's eye the algebraic equation of Snow, the equals sign, and the answer in the man before me.

"Snow is my last name," said George. He swung into the saddle and they started cautiously out into the darkening swirl of fresh new currency just issuing from the Snowdrop Mint. The girl, to keep her place, clung happily to the sturdy figure of the camp cook.

I brought three things away from Ross Curtis's ranch house--yea, four. One was the appreciation of snow, which I have so humbly tried here to render; (2) was a collarbone, of which I am extra careful;

(3) was a memory of what it is to eat very extremely terribly bad food for a week; and (4) was the cause of (3) a little note delivered at the end of the week and hand-painted in blue pencil on a sheet of meat paper.

"I cannot come back there to that there job. Mrs. Snow say no, George. I been revolvin' it in my mind; considerin' circumstances she's right."[9]

Editorial Note: Before the fatal illness of William Sydney Porter (known through his literary work as "O. Henry") this American master of short-story writing had begun for Hamp-

---

[9] this story appeared in the posthumous collection, Waifs and Strays, 1917

ton's Magazine the story printed below. Illness crept upon him rapidly and he was compelled to give up writing about at the point where the girl enters the story.

When he realized that he could do no more (it was his lifelong habit to write with a pencil, never dictating to a stenographer), O. Henry told in detail the remainder of The Snow Man to Harris Merton Lyon, whom he had often spoken of as one of the most effective short-story writers of the present time. Mr. Porter had delineated all of the characters, leaving only the rounding out of the plot in the final pages to Mr. Lyon.

XIV A Visit from Saint Nicholas

IN THE ERNEST HEMINGWAY MANNER[10]
By James Thurber

IT WAS the night before Christmas. The house was very quiet. No creatures were stirring in the house. There weren't even any mice stirring. The stockings had been hung carefully by the chimney. The children hoped that Saint Nicholas would come and fill them.

The children were in their beds. Their beds were in the room next to ours. Mamma and I were in our beds. Mamma wore a kerchief. I had my cap on. I could hear the children moving. We didn't move. We wanted the children to think we were asleep.

"Father," the children said.

There was no answer. He's there, all right, they thought.

"Father," they said, and banged on their beds.

"What do you want?" I asked.

"We have visions of sugarplums," the children said.

"Go to sleep," said mamma.

"We can't sleep," said the children. They stopped talking, but I could hear them moving. They made sounds.

"Can you sleep?" asked the children.

"No," I said.

"You ought to sleep."

"I know. I ought to sleep."

"Can we have some sugarplums?"

"You can't have any sugarplums," said mamma.

"We just asked you."

There was a long silence. I could hear the children moving again.

---

[10] from The New Yorker, December 24, 1927

"Is Saint Nicholas asleep?" asked the children.

"No," mamma said. "Be quiet."

"What the hell would he be asleep tonight for?" I asked.

"He might be," the children said.

"He isn't," I said.

"Let's try to sleep," said mamma.

The house became quiet once more. I could hear the rustling noises the children made when they moved in their beds.

Out on the lawn a clatter arose. I got out of bed and went to the window. I opened the shutters; then I threw up the sash. The moon shone on the snow. The moon gave the lustre of mid-day to objects in the snow. There was a miniature sleigh in the snow, and eight tiny reindeer. A little man was driving them. He was lively and quick. He whistled and shouted at the reindeer and called them by their names. Their names were Dasher, Dancer, Prancer, Vixen, Comet, Cupid, Donder, and Blitzen.

He told them to dash away to the top of the porch, and then he told them to dash away to the top of the wall. They did. The sleigh was full of toys.

"Who is it?" mamma asked.

"Some guy," I said. "A little guy."

I pulled my head in out of the window and listened. I heard the reindeer on the roof. I could hear their hoofs pawing and prancing on the roof. "Shut the window," said mamma. I stood still and listened.

"What do you hear?"

"Reindeer," I said. I shut the window and walked about. It was cold. Mamma sat up in the bed and looked at me.

"How would they get on the roof?" mamma asked.

"They fly."

"Get into bed. You'll catch cold."

Mamma lay down in bed. I didn't get into bed. I kept walking around.

"What do you mean, they fly?" asked mamma.

"Just fly is all."

Mamma turned away toward the wall. She didn't say anything.

I went out into the room where the chimney was. The little man came down the chimney and stepped into the room. He was dressed all in fur. His clothes were covered with ashes and soot from the chimney. On his back was a pack like a peddler's pack. There were toys in it. His cheeks and nose were red and he had dimples. His eyes twinkled. His mouth was little, like a bow, and his beard was very white. Between his teeth was a stumpy pipe. The smoke from the pipe encircled his head in a wreath. He laughed and his belly shook. It shook like a bowl of red jelly. I laughed. He winked his eye, then he gave a twist to his head. He didn't say anything.

He turned to the chimney and filled the stockings and turned away from the chimney. Laying his finger aside his nose, he gave a nod. Then he went up the chimney. I went to the chimney and looked up. I saw him get into his sleigh. He whistled at his team and the team flew away. The team flew as lightly as thistledown. The driver called out, "Merry Christmas and good night." I went back to bed.

"What was it?" asked mamma. "Saint Nicholas?" She smiled.

"Yeah," I said.

She sighed and turned in the bed.

"I saw him," I said.

"Sure."

"I did see him."

"Sure you saw him." She turned farther toward the wall.

"Father," said the children.

"There you go," mamma said. "You and your flying reindeer."

"Go to sleep," I said.

"Can we see Saint Nicholas when he comes?" the children asked.

"You got to be asleep," I said. "You got to be asleep when he comes. You can't see him unless you're unconscious."

"Father knows," mamma said.

I pulled the covers over my mouth. It was warm under the covers. As I went to sleep I wondered if mamma was right.[11]

---

[11] Copyright 1927, James Thurber, but never collected, and copyright was not renewed in a timely fashion, so now in public domain.

XV An Unfinished Christmas Story
By O. Henry

Now, a Christmas story should be one. For a good many years the ingenious writers have been putting forth tales for the holiday numbers that employed every subtle, evasive, indirect, and strategic scheme they could invent to disguise the Christmas flavor. So far has this new practice been carried that nowadays when you read a story in a holiday magazine the only way you can tell it is a Christmas story is to look at the footnote which reads: ["The incidents in the above story happened on December 25th.--ED."]

There is progress in this; but it is all very sad. There are just as many real Christmas stories as ever, if we would only dig 'em up. Me, I am for the Scrooge and Marley Christmas story, and the Annie and Willie's prayer poem, and the long lost son coming home on the stroke of twelve to the poorly thatched cottage with his arms full of talking dolls and popcorn balls and--Zip! you hear the second mortgage on the cottage go flying off it into the deep snow.

So, this is to warn you that there is no subterfuge about this story--and you might come upon stockings hung to the mantel and plum puddings and hark! the chimes! and wealthy misers loosening up and handing over penny whistles to lame newsboys if you read further.

Once I knocked at a door (I have so many things to tell you I keep on losing sight of the story). It was the front door of a furnished room house in West 'Teenth Street. I was looking for a young illustrator named Paley originally and irrevocably from Terre Haute. Paley doesn't enter even into the first serial rights of this Christmas story; I mention him simply in explaining why I came to knock at the door--some people have so much curiosity.

The door was opened by the landlady. I had seen hundreds like her. And I had smelled before that cold, dank, furnished draught of air that hurried by her to escape immurement in the furnished house.

She was stout, and her face and hands were as white as though she had been drowned in a barrel of vinegar. One hand held together at her throat a buttonless flannel dressing sacque whose lines had been cut by no tape or butterick known to mortal woman. Beneath this a too long, flowered, black sateen skirt was draped about her, reaching the floor in stiff wrinkles and folds.

The rest of her was yellow. Her hair, in some bygone age, had been dipped in the fountain of folly presided over by the merry nymph Hydrogen; but now, except at the roots, it had returned to its natural grim and grizzled white.

Her eyes and teeth and finger nails were yellow. Her chops hung low and shook when she moved. The look on her face was exactly that smileless look of fatal melancholy that you may have seen on the countenance of a hound left sitting on the doorstep of a deserted cabin.

I inquired for Paley. After a long look of cold suspicion the landlady spoke, and her voice matched the dingy roughness of her flannel sacque.

Paley? Was I sure that was the name? And wasn't it, likely, Mr. Sanderson I meant, in the third floor rear? No; it was Paley I wanted. Again that frozen, shrewd, steady study of my soul from her pale-yellow, unwinking eyes, trying to penetrate my mask of deception and rout out my true motives from my lying lips. There was a Mr. Tompkins in the front hall bedroom two flights up. Perhaps it

212

was he I was seeking. He worked of nights; he never came in till seven in the morning. Or if it was really Mr. Tucker (thinly disguised as Paley) that I was hunting I would have to call between five and--But no; I held firmly to Paley. There was no such name among her lodgers. Click! the door closed swiftly in my face; and I heard through the panels the clanking of chains and bolts.

I went down the steps and stopped to consider. The number of this house was 43. I was sure Paley had said 43--or perhaps it was 45 or 47--I decided to try 47, the second house farther along.

I rang the bell. The door opened; and there stood the same woman. I wasn't confronted by just a resemblance--it was the *same* woman holding together the same old sacque at her throat and looking at me with the same yellow eyes as if she had never seen me before on earth. I saw on the knuckle of her second finger the same red-and-black spot made, probably, by a recent burn against a hot stove.

I stood speechiess and gaping while one with moderate haste might have told fifty. I couldn't have spoken Paley's name even if I had remembered it. I did the only thing that a brave man who believes there are mysterious forces in nature that we do not yet fully comprehend could have done in the circumstances. I backed down the steps to the sidewalk and then hurried away frontward, fully under-standing how incidents like that must bother the psychical research people and the census takers.

Of course I heard an explanation of it afterward, as we always do about inexplicable things.

The landlady was Mrs. Kannon; and she leased three adjoining houses, which she made into one by cutting arched doorways through the wails. She sat in the middle house and answered the three bells.

I wonder why I have maundered so slowly through the prologue. I have it! it was simply to say to you, in the form of introduction rife through the Middle West: "Shake hands with Mrs. Kannon."

For, it was in her triple house that the Christmas story happened; and it was there where I picked up the incontrovertible facts from the gossip of many roomers and met Stickney--and saw the necktie.

Christmas came that year on Thursday, and snow came with it.

Stickney (Harry Clarence Fowler Stickney to whomsoever his full baptismal cognominal burdens may be of interest) reached his address at six-thirty Wednesday afternoon. "Address" is New Yorkese for "Home." Stickney roomed at 45 West 'Teenth Street, third floor rear hall room. He was twenty years and four months old, and he worked in a cameras-of-all-kinds, photographic supplies and films-developed store. I don't know what kind of work he did in the store; but you must have seen him. He is the young man who always comes behind the counter to wait on you and lets you talk for five minutes, telling him what you want. When you are done, he calls the proprietor at the top of his voice to wait on you, and walks away whistling between his teeth.

I don't want to bother about describing to you his appearance; but, if you are a man reader, I will say that Stickney looked precisely like the young chap that you always find sitting in your chair smoking a cigarette after you have missed a shot while playing pool--not billiards, but pool--when you want to sit down yourself.

There are some to whom Christmas gives no Christmassy essence. Of course, prosperous people and comfortable people who have homes or flats or rooms

214

with meals, and even people who live in apartment houses with hotel service get something of the Christmas flavor. They give one another presents with the cost mark scratched off with a penknife; and they hang holly wreaths in the front windows, and when they are asked whether they prefer light or dark meat from the turkey they say: "Both, please," and giggle and have lots of fun. And the very poorest people have the best time of it. The Army gives 'em a dinner, and the 10 A.M. issue of the Night Final edition of the newspaper with the largest circulation in the city leaves a basket at their door full of an apple, a Lake Ronkonkoma squab, a scrambled eggplant, and a bunch of Kalamazoo bleached parsley. The poorer you are the more Christmas does for you.

But, I'll tell you to what kind of a mortal Christmas seems to be only the day before the twenty-sixth day of December. It's the chap in the big city earning sixteen dollars a week, with no friends and few acquaintances, who finds himself with only fifty cents in his pocket on Christmas eve. He can't accept charity; he can't borrow; he knows no one who would invite him to dinner. I have a fancy that when the shepherds left their flocks to follow the star of Bethlehem there was a bandy-legged young fellow among them who was just learning the sheep business. So they said to him, "Bobby, we're going to investigate this star route and see what's in it. If it should turn out to be the first Christmas day we don't want to miss it. And, as you are not a wise man, and as you couldn't possibly purchase a present to take along, suppose you stay behind and mind the sheep." So as we may say, Harry Stickney was a direct descendant of the shepherd who was left behind to take care of the flocks.

Getting back to facts, Stickney rang the door-bell of 45.

He had a habit of forgetting his latchkey.

Instantly the door opened and there stood Mrs. Kannon, clutching her sacque together at the throat and gorgonizing him with her opaque yellow eyes.

(To give you good measure, here is a story within a story. Once a roomer in 47 who had a Scotch habit, not kilts, but a habit of drinking Scotch--began to figure to himself what might happen if two persons should ring the doorbells of 43 and 47 at the same time. Visions of two halves of Mrs. Kannon appearing respectively and simultaneously at the two entrances, each clutching at a side of an open, flapping sacque that could never meet, overpowered him. Bellevue got him.)

"Evening," said Stickney cheerlessly, as he distributed little piles of muddy slush along the hall matting. "Think we'll have snow?" "You left your key," said-- (Here the manuscript ends.)

XVI Whistling Dick's Christmas Stocking

By O. Henry

It was with much caution that Whistling Dick slid back
the door of the box-car, for Article 5716, City Ordinances,
authorized (perhaps unconstitutionally) arrest on suspicion, and he was familiar of old with this ordinance. So,
before climbing out, he surveyed the field with all the care
of a good general.

He saw no change since his last visit to this big, alms-
giving, long-suffering city of the South, the cold weather
paradise of the tramps. The levee where his freight-car
stood was pimpled with dark bulks of merchandise. The
breeze reeked with the well-remembered, sickening smell
of the old tarpaulins that covered bales and barrels.

The dun river slipped along among the shipping with
an oily gurgle. Far down toward Chalmette he could see
the great bend in the stream, outlined by the row of electric lights. Across the river Algiers lay, a long, irregular
blot, made darker by the dawn which lightened the sky
beyond. An industrious tug or two, coming for some early
sailing ship, gave a few appalling toots, that seemed to be
the signal for breaking day. The Italian luggers were
creeping nearer their landing, laden with early vegetables
and shellfish. A vague roar, subterranean in quality, from
dray wheels and street cars, began to make itself heard
and felt; and the ferryboats, the Mary Anns of water craft,
stirred sullenly to their menial morning tasks.

Whistling Dick's red head popped suddenly back into
the car. A sight too imposing and magnificent for his gaze
had been added to the scene. A vast, incomparable po-

liceman rounded a pile of rice sacks and stood within twenty yards of the car. The daily miracle of the dawn, now being performed above Algiers, received the flattering attention of this specimen of municipal official splendor. He gazed with unbiased dignity at the faintly glowing colors until, at last, he turned to them his broad back, as if convinced that legal interference was not needed, and the sunrise might proceed unchecked. So he turned his face to the rice bags, and, drawing a flat flask from an inside pocket, he placed it to his lips and regarded the firmament.

Whistling Dick, professional tramp, possessed a half-friendly acquaintance with this officer. They had met several times before on the levee at night, for the officer, himself a lover of music, had been attracted by the exquisite whistling of the shiftless vagabond. Still, he did not care, under the present circumstances, to renew the acquaintance. There is a difference between meeting a policeman upon a lonely wharf and whistling a few operatic airs with him, and being caught by him crawling out of a freight-car. So Dick waited, as even a New Orleans policeman must move on some time--perhaps it is a retributive law of nature--and before long "Big Fritz" majestically disappeared between the trains of cars.

Whistling Dick waited as long as his judgment advised, and then slid swiftly to the ground. Assuming as far as possible the air of an honest laborer who seeks his daily toil, he moved across the network of railway lines, with the intention of making his way by quiet Girod Street to a certain bench in Lafayette Square, where, according to appointment, he hoped to rejoin a pal known as "Slick," this adventurous pilgrim having preceded him by one day in a cattle-car into which a loose slat had enticed him.

As Whistling Dick picked his way where night still lingered among the big, reeking, musty warehouses, he gave way to the habit that had won for him his title. Subdued, yet clear, with each note as true and liquid as a bobolink's, his whistle tinkled about the dim, cold mountains of brick like drops of rain falling into a hidden pool. He followed an air, but it swam mistily into a swirling current of improvisation. You could cull out the trill of mountain brooks, the staccato of green rushes shivering above the chilly lagoons, the pipe of sleepy birds.

Rounding a corner, the whistler collided with a mountain of blue and brass.

"So," observed the mountain calmly, "you are already pack. Und dere vill not pe frost before two veeks yet! Und you haf forgotten how to vistle. Dere was a valse note in dot last bar."

"Watcher know about it?" said Whistling Dick, with tentative familiarity; "you wit yer little Gherman-band nixcumrous chunes. Watcher know about music? Pick yer ears, and listen agin. Here's de way I whistled it--see?"

He puckered his lips, but the big policeman held up his hand.

"Shtop," he said, "und learn der right way. Und learn also dot a rolling shtone can't vistle for a cent."

Big Fritz's heavy moustache rounded into a circle, and from its depths came a sound deep and mellow as that from a flute. He repeated a few bars of the air the tramp had been whistling. The rendition was cold, but correct, and he emphasized the note he had taken exception to.

"Dot p is p natural, and not p vlat. Py der vay, you petter pe glad I meet you. Von hour later, und I vould haf to put you in a gage to vistle mit der chail pirds. Der orders are to bull all der pums after sunrise."

"To which?"

"To bull der pums--eferybody mitout fisible means. Dirty days is der price, or fifteen tollars."

"Is dat straight, or a game you givin' me?"

"It's der pest tip you efer had. I gif it to you pecause I pelief you are not so bad as der rest. Und pecause you can vistle 'Der Freischütz' bezzer dan I myself gan. Don't run against any more bolicemans aroundt der corners, but go away from town a few tays. Goot-pye."

So Madame Orleans had at last grown weary of the strange and ruffled brood that came yearly to nestle beneath her charitable pinions.

After the big policeman had departed, Whistling Dick stood for an irresolute minute, feeling all the outraged indignation of a delinquent tenant who is ordered to vacate his premises. He had pictured to himself a day of dreamful ease when he should have joined his pal; a day of lounging on the wharf, munching the bananas and cocoanuts scattered in unloading the fruit steamers; and then a feast along the free-lunch counters from which the easy-going owners were too good-natured or too generous to drive him away, and afterward a pipe in one of the little flowery parks and a snooze in some shady corner of the wharf. But here was a stern order to exile, and one that he knew must be obeyed. So, with a wary eye open for the gleam of brass buttons, he began his retreat toward a rural refuge. A few days in the country need not necessarily prove disastrous. Beyond the possibility of a slight nip of frost, there was no formidable evil to be looked for.

However, it was with a depressed spirit that Whistling Dick passed the old French market on his chosen route down the river. For safety's sake he still presented to the world his portrayal of the part of the worthy artisan on his way to labor. A stall-keeper in the market, undeceived, hailed him by the generic name of his ilk, and "Jack" halted, taken by surprise. The vendor, melted by this proof of his own acuteness, bestowed a foot of Frankfurter and half a loaf, and thus the problem of breakfast was solved.

When the streets, from topographical reasons, began to shun the river bank the exile mounted to the top of the levee, and on its well-trodden path pursued his way. The suburban eye regarded him with cold suspicion; individuals reflected the stern spirit of the city's heartless edict. He missed the seclusion of the crowded town and the safety he could always find in the multitude.

At Chalmette, six miles upon his desultory way, there suddenly menaced him a vast and bewildering industry. A new port was being established; the dock was being built, compresses were going up; picks and shovels and harrows struck at him like serpents from every side. An arrogant foreman bore down upon him, estimating his muscles with the eye of a recruiting-sergeant. Brown men and black men all about him were toiling away. He fled in terror.

By noon he had reached the country of the plantations, the great, sad, silent levels bordering the mighty river. He overlooked fields of sugarcane so vast that their farthest limits melted into the sky. The sugar-making season was well advanced, and the cutters were at work; the wagons creaked drearily after them; the Negro teamsters inspired the mules to greater speed with mellow and sonorous imprecations. Dark-green groves, blurred by the blue of distance, showed where the plantation-houses stood. The tall chimneys of the sugar-mills caught the eye miles distant, like lighthouses at sea.

At a certain point Whistling Dick's unerring nose

caught the scent of frying fish. Like a pointer to a quail, he made his way down the levee side straight to the camp of a credulous and ancient fisherman, whom he charmed with song and story, so that he dined like an admiral, and then like a philosopher annihilated the worst three hours of the day by a nap under the trees.

When he awoke and again continued his hegira, a frosty sparkle in the air succeeded the drowsy warmth of the day, and as this portent of a chilly night translated itself to the brain of Sir Peregrine, he lengthened his stride and bethought him of shelter. He traveled a road that faithfully followed the convolutions of the levee, running along its base, but whither he knew not. Bushes and rank grass crowded it to the wheel ruts, and out of this ambuscade the pests of the lowlands swarmed after him, humming a keen vicious soprano. And as the night grew nearer, although colder, the whine of the mosquitoes became a greedy, petulant snarl that shut out all other sounds.

To his right, against the heavens, he saw a green light moving, and, accompanying it, the masts and funnels of a big incoming steamer, moving as upon a screen at a magic-lantern show. And there were mysterious marshes at his left, out of which came queer gurgling cries and a choked croaking. The whistling vagrant struck up a merry warble to offset these melancholy influences, and it is likely that never before, since Pan himself jiggered it on his reeds, had such sounds been heard in those depressing solitudes.

A distant clatter in the rear quickly developed into the swift beat of horses' hoofs, and Whistling Dick stepped aside into the dew-wet grass to clear the track. Turning his head, he saw approaching a fine team of stylish grays drawing a double surrey. A stout man with a white moustache occupied the front seat, giving all his attention to the rigid lines in his hands. Behind him sat a placid, middle-aged lady and a brilliant-looking girl hardly arrived at young ladyhood. The lap-robe had slipped partly from the knees of the gentleman driving, and Whistling Dick saw two stout canvas bags between his feet--bags such as, while loafing in cities, he had seen warily transferred between express wagons and bank doors. The remaining space in the vehicle was filled with parcels of various sizes and shapes.

As the surrey swept even with the sidetracked tramp, the bright-eyed girl, seized by some merry, madcap impulse, leaned out toward him with a sweet, dazzling smile, and cried, "Mer-ry Christ-mas!" in a shrill, plaintive treble.

Such a thing had not often happened to Whistling Dick, and he felt handicapped in devising the correct response. But lacking time for reflection, he let his instinct decide, and snatching off his battered derby, he rapidly extended it at arm's length, and drew it back with a continuous motion, and shouted a loud, but ceremonious, "Ah, there!" after the flying surrey.

The sudden movement of the girl had caused one of the parcels to become unwrapped, and something limp and black fell from it into the road. The tramp picked it up and found it to be a new black silk stocking, long and fine and slender. It crunched crisply, and yet with a luxurious softness, between his fingers.

"Ther bloomin' little skeezicks!" said Whistling Dick, with a broad grin bisecting his freckled face. "Wot d'yer think of dat, now! Mer-ry Chris-mus! Sounded like a cuckoo clock, dat's what she did. Dem guys is swells, too, bet yer life, an' der old 'un stacks dem sacks of dough down under his trotters like dey was common as dried

apples. Been shoppin' fer Chrismus, and de kid's lost one
of her new socks w'ot she was goin' to hold up Santy wid.
De bloomin' little skeezicks! Wit' her 'Mer-ry Chris-mus!'
W'ot 'd yer t'ink! Same as to say, 'Hello, Jack, how goes it?'
and as swell as Fift' Av'noo, and as easy as a blowout in
Cincinnat'."

Whistling Dick folded the stocking carefully and stuffed
it into his pocket.

It was nearly two hours later when he came upon signs
of habitation. The buildings of an extensive plantation
were brought into view by a turn in the road. He easily se-
lected the planter's residence in a large square building
with two wings, with numerous good-sized, well-lighted
windows, and broad verandas running around its full extent. It was set upon a smooth lawn, which was faintly lit
by the far-reaching rays of the lamps within. A noble
grove surrounded it, and old-fashioned shrubbery grew
thickly about the walls and fences. The quarters of the
hands and the mill buildings were situated at a distance in
the rear.

The road was now enclosed on each side by a fence, and
presently, as Whistling Dick drew nearer the houses, he
suddenly stopped and sniffed the air.

"If dere ain't a hobo stew cookin' somewhere in dis immediate precinct," he said to himself, "me nose has quit
tellin' de trut'."

Without hesitation he climbed the fence to windward.
He found himself in an apparently disused lot, where piles
of old bricks were stacked, and rejected, decaying lumber.
In a corner he saw the faint glow of a fire that had become
little more than a bed of living coals, and he thought he
could see some dim human forms sitting or lying about it.
He drew nearer, and by the light of a little blaze that sud-

denly flared up he saw plainly the fat figure of a ragged man in an old brown sweater and cap.

"Dat man," said Whistling Dick to himself softly, "is a dead ringer for Boston Harry. I'll try him wit' de high sign."

He whistled one or two bars of a rag-time melody, and the air was immediately taken up, and then quickly ended with a peculiar run. The first whistler walked confidently up to the fire. The fat man looked up and spake in a loud, asthmatic wheeze:

"Gents, the unexpected but welcome addition to our circle is Mr. Whistling Dick, an old friend of mine for whom I fully vouches. The waiter will lay another cover at once. Mr. W. D. will join us at supper, during which function he will enlighten us in regard to the circumstances that give us the pleasure of his company."

"Chewin' de stuffin' out'n de dictionary, as usual, Boston," said Whistling Dick; "but t'anks all de same for de invitashun. I guess I finds self here about de same way as yous guys. A cop gimme de tip dis mornin'. Yous workin' on dis farm?"

"A guest," said Boston sternly, "shouldn't never insult his entertainers until he's filled up wid grub. 'Tain't good business sense. Workin'!--but I will restrain myself. We five--me, Deaf Pete, Blinky, Goggles, and Indiana Tom--got put on to this scheme of Noo Orleans to work visiting gentlemen upon her dirty streets, and we hit the road last evening just as the tender hues of twilight had flopped down upon the daisies and things. Blinky, pass the empty oyster-can at your left to the empty gentleman at your right."

For the next ten minutes the gang of roadsters paid their undivided attention to the supper. In an old five-gallon kerosene can they had cooked a stew of potatoes, meat, and onions which they partook of from smaller cans they had found scattered about the vacant lot.

Whistling Dick had known Boston Harry of old, and knew him to be one of the shrewdest and most successful of his brotherhood. He looked like a prosperous stock-drover or a solid merchant from some country village. He was stout and hale, with a ruddy, always smoothly shaven face. His clothes were strong and neat, and he gave special attention to his decent-appearing shoes. During the past ten years he had acquired a reputation for working a lar-ger number of successfully managed confidence games than any of his acquaintances, and he had not a day's work to be counted against him. It was rumored among his as-sociates that he had saved a considerable amount of money. The four other men were fair specimens of the slinking, ill-clad, noisome genus who carried their labels of "suspicious" in plain view.

After the bottom of the large can had been scraped, and pipes lit at the coals, two of the men called Boston aside and spake with him lowly and mysteriously. He nodded decisively, and then said aloud to Whistling Dick:

"Listen, sonny, to some plain talky-talk. We five are on a lay. I've guaranteed you to be square, and you're to come in on the profits equal with the boys, and you've got to help. Two hundred hands on this plantation are expecting to be paid a week's wages to-morrow morning. Tomor-row's Christmas, and they want to lay off. Says the boss: 'Work from five to nine in the morning to get a train load of sugar off, and I'll pay every man cash down for the week and a day extra.' They say: 'Hooray for the boss! It goes.' He drives to Noo Orleans to-day, and fetches back the cold dollars. Two thousand and seventy-four fifty is the amount. I got the figures from a man who talks too much, who got 'em from the bookkeeper. The boss of this plantation thinks he's going to pay this wealth to the hands. He's got it down wrong; he's going to pay it to us. It's going to stay in the leisure class, where it belongs. Now, half of this haul goes to me, and the other half the rest of you may divide.

Why the difference? I represent the brains. It's my scheme. Here's the way we're going to get it. There's some company at supper in the house, but they'll leave about nine. They've just happened in for an hour or so. If they don't go pretty soon, we'll work the scheme anyhow. We want all night to get away good with the dollars. They're heavy. About nine o'clock Dear Pete and Blinky'll go down the road about a quarter beyond the house, and set fire to a big cane-field there that the cutters haven't touched yet. The wind's just right to have it roaring in two minutes. The alarm'll be given, and every man Jack about the place will be down there in ten minutes, fighting fire. That'll leave the money sacks and the women alone in the house for us to handle. You've heard cane burn? Well, there's mighty few women can screech loud enough to be heard above its crackling. The thing's dead safe. The only danger is in being caught before we can get far enough away with the money. Now, if you--"

"Boston," interrupted Whistling Dick, rising to his feet, "t'anks for de grub yous fellers has given me, but I'll be movin' on now."

"What do you mean?" asked Boston, also rising.

"W'y, you can count me outer dis deal. You oughter know that. I'm on de bum all right enough, but dat other t'ing don't go wit' me. Burglary is no good. I'll say good night and many t'anks fer--"

Whistling Dick had moved away a few steps as he spoke, but he stopped very suddenly. Boston had covered him with a short revolver of roomy calibre.

"Take your seat," said the tramp leader. "I'd feel mighty proud of myself if I let you go and spoil the game. You'll stick right in this camp until we finish the job. The end of that brick pile is your limit. You go two inches beyond that, and I'll have to shoot. Better take it easy, now."

"It's my way of doin'," said Whistling Dick. "Easy goes. You can depress de muzzle of dat twelve-incher, and run 'em back on de trucks. I remains, as de newspapers says, 'in yer midst.'"

"All right," said Boston, lowering his piece, as the other returned and took his seat again on a projecting plank in a pile of timber. "Don't try to leave; that's all. I wouldn't miss this chance even if I had to shoot an old acquaintance to make it go. I don't want to hurt anybody specially, but this thousand dollars I'm going to get will fix me for fair. I'm going to drop the road, and start a saloon in a little town I know about. I'm tired of being kicked around."

Boston Harry took from his pocket a cheap silver watch and held it near the fire.

"It's a quarter to nine," he said. "Pete, you and Blinky start. Go down the road past the house and fire the cane in a dozen places. Then strike for the levee, and come back on it, instead of the road, so you won't meet anybody. By the time you get back the men will all be striking out for the fire, and we'll break for the house and collar the dollars. Everybody cough up what matches he's got."

The two surly tramps made a collection of all the matches in the party, Whistling Dick contributing his quota with propitiatory alacrity, and then they departed in the dim starlight in the direction of the road.

Of the three remaining vagrants, two, Goggles and Indiana Tom, reclined lazily upon convenient lumber and regarded Whistling Dick with undisguised disfavor. Boston, observing that the dissenting recruit was disposed to remain peaceably, relaxed a little of his vigilance. Whistling Dick arose presently and strolled leisurely up and down keeping carefully within the territory assigned him.

"Dis planter chap," he said, pausing before Boston Harry, "w'ot makes yer t'ink he's got de tin in de house wit' 'im?"

"I'm advised of the facts in the case," said Boston. "He drove to Noo Orleans and got it, I say, to-day. Want to change your mind now and come in?"

"Naw, I was just askin'. Wot kind o' team did de boss drive?"

"Pair of grays."

"Double surrey?"

"Women folks along?"

"Wife and kid. Say, what morning paper are you trying to pump news for?"

"I was just conversin' to pass de time away. I guess dat team passed me in de road dis evenin'. Dat's all."

As Whistling Dick put his hands into his pockets and continued his curtailed beat up and down by the fire, he felt the silk stocking he had picked up in the road.

"Ther bloomin' little skeezicks," he muttered, with a grin.

As he walked up and down he could see, through a sort of natural opening or lane among the trees, the planter's residence some seventy-five yards distant. The side of the house toward him exhibited spacious, well-lighted windows through which a soft radiance streamed, illuminating the broad veranda and some extent of the lawn beneath.

"What's that you said?" asked Boston, sharply.

"Oh, nuttin' 't all," said Whistling Dick, lounging care-lessly, and kicking meditatively at a little stone on the ground.

"Just as easy," continued the warbling vagrant softly to himself, "an' sociable an' swell, an' sassy, wit' her 'Mer-ry Chris-mus.' Wot d'yer t'ink, now!"

Dinner, two hours late, was being served in the Belle-meade plantation dining-room.

The dining-room and all its appurtenances spoke of an old r'gime that was here continued rather than suggested to the memory. The plate was rich to the extent that its age and quaintness alone saved it from being showy; there were interesting names signed in the corners of the pic-tures on the walls; the viands were of the kind that bring a shine into the eyes of gourmets. The service was swift, si-lent, lavish, as in the days when the waiters were assets like the plate. The names by which the planter's family and their visitors addressed one another were historic in the annals of two nations. Their manners and conversation had that most difficult kind of ease--the kind that still pre-serves punctilio. The planter himself seemed to be the dynamo that generated the larger portion of the gaiety and wit. The younger ones at the board found it more than dif-ficult to turn back on him his guns of raillery and banter. It is true, the young men attempted to storm his works re-peatedly, incited by the hope of gaining the approbation of their fair companions; but even when they sped a well-aimed shaft, the planter forced them to feel defeat by the tremendous discomfiting thunder of the laughter with which he accompanied his retorts. At the head of the table, serene, matronly, benevolent, reigned the mistress of the house, placing here and there the right smile, the right word, the encouraging glance.

The talk of the party was too desultory, too evanescent to follow, but at last they came to the subject of the tramp nuisance, one that had of late vexed the plantations for many miles around. The planter seized the occasion to direct his good-natured fire of raillery at the mistress, accusing her of encouraging the plague. "They swarm up and down the river every winter," he said. "They overrun New Orleans, and we catch the surplus, which is generally the worst part.

And, a day or two ago, Madame New Orleans, suddenly discovering that she can't go shopping without brushing her skirts against great rows of the vagabonds sunning themselves on the banquettes, says to the police: 'Catch 'em all,' and the police catch a dozen or two, and the remaining three or four thousand overflow up and down the levees, and madame there"--pointing tragically with the carving-knife at her--"feeds them. They won't work, they defy my overseers, and they make friends with my dogs; and you, madame, feed them before my eyes, and intimidate me when I would interfere. Tell us, please, how many to-day did you thus incite to future laziness and depredation?"

"Six, I think," said madame, with a reflective smile; "but you know two of them offered to work, for you heard them yourself."

The planter's disconcerting laugh rang out again.

"Yes, at their own trades. And one was an artificial-flower maker, and the other a glass-blower. Oh, they were looking for work! Not a hand would they consent to lift to labor of any other kind."

"And another one," continued the soft-hearted mistress,

231

"used quite good language. It was really extraordinary for one of his class. And he carried a watch. And had lived in Boston. I don't believe they are all bad. They have always seemed to me to rather lack development. I always look upon them as children with whom wisdom has remained at a standstill while whiskers have continued to grow. We passed one this evening as we were driving home who had a face as good as it was incompetent. He was whistling the intermezzo from 'Cavalleria' and blowing the spirit of Mascagni himself into it."

A bright-eyed young girl who sat at the left of the mistress leaned over and said in a confidential undertone:

"I wonder, Mamma, if that tramp we passed on the road found my stocking, and do you think he will hang it up to-night? Now I can hang up but one. Do you know why I wanted a new pair of silk stockings when I have plenty? Well, old Aunt Judy says, if you hang up two that have never been worn, Santa Claus will fill one with good things, and Monsieur Pambe will place in the other payment for all the words you have spoken--good or bad--on the day before Christmas. That's why I've been unusually nice and polite to everyone to-day. Monsieur Pambe, you know, is a witch gentleman! he--"

The words of the young girl were interrupted by a startling thing.

Like the wraith of some burned-out shooting star, a black streak came crashing through the window-pane and upon the table, where it shivered into fragments a dozen pieces of crystal and china ware, and then glanced between the heads of the guests to the wall, imprinting therein a deep, round indentation, at which, to-day, the visitor to Bellemeade marvels as he gazes upon it and listens to this tale as it is told.

The women screamed in many keys, and the men sprang to their feet, and would have laid their hands upon their swords had not the verities of chronology forbidden.

The planter was the first to act; he sprang to the intruding missile and held it up to view.

"By Jupiter!" he cried. "A meteoric shower of hosiery! Has communication at last been established with Mars?"

"I should say--ahem!--Venus," ventured a young gentleman visitor, looking hopefully for approbation toward the unresponsive young-lady visitors.

The planter held at arm's length the unceremonious visitor--a long dangling black stocking. "It's loaded," he announced.

As he spoke he reversed the stocking, holding it by the toe, and down from it dropped a roundish stone, wrapped about by a piece of yellowish paper. "Now for the first interstellar message of the century!" he cried; and nodding to the company, who had crowded about him, he adjusted his glasses with provoking deliberation, and examined it closely. When he finished he had changed from the jolly host to the practical, decisive man of business. He immediately struck a bell, and said to the silent-footed mulatto man who responded: "Go and tell Mr. Wesley to get Reeves and Maurice and about ten stout hands they can rely upon, and come to the hall door at once. Tell him to have the men arm themselves, and bring plenty of ropes and plough lines. Tell him to hurry." And then he read aloud from the paper these words:

To the Gent of de Hous:

Dere is five tuff hoboes xcept meself in the vaken lot near de road war de old brick piles is. Dey got me stuck up wid a gun see and I taken dis means of comunikaten. 2 of der lads is gone down to set fire to de cain field below de hous and when yous fellers goes to turn de hoes on it de hole gang is goin to rob de house of de money yoo gotto pay off wit say git a move on ye say de kid dropt dis sock in der rode tel her mery crismus de same as she told me. Ketch de bums down de rode first and den sen a relefe core to get me out of soke youres truly,

Whistlen Dick

There was some quiet, but rapid, maneuvering at Belle-meade during the ensuing half hour, which ended in five disgusted and sullen tramps being captured and locked securely in an out-house pending the coming of the morning and retribution. For another result, the visiting young gentlemen had secured the unqualified worship of the visiting young ladies by their distinguished and heroic conduct.

For still another, behold Whistling Dick, the hero, seated at the planter's table, feasting upon viands his experience had never before included, and waited upon by admiring femininity in shapes of such beauty and "swell-ness" that even his ever-full mouth could scarcely prevent him from whistling. He was made to disclose in detail his adventure with the evil gang of Boston Harry, and how he cunningly wrote the note and wrapped it around the stone and placed it in the toe of the stocking, and, watching his chance, sent it silently, with a wonderful centrifugal momentum, like a comet, at one of the big lighted windows of the dining-room.

The planter vowed that the wanderer should wander no more; that his was a goodness and an honesty that should be rewarded, and that a debt of gratitude had been made that must be paid; for had he not saved them from a doubtless imminent loss, and maybe a greater calamity? He assured Whistling Dick that he might consider himself a charge upon the honor of Bellemeade; that a position suited to his powers would be found for him at once, and hinted that the way would be heartily smoothed for him to rise to as high places of emolument and trust as the plantation afforded.

But now, they said, he must be weary, and the immediate thing to consider was rest and sleep. So the mistress spoke to a servant, and Whistling Dick was conducted to a room in the wing of the house occupied by the servants. To this room, in a few minutes, was brought a portable tin bathtub filled with water, which was placed on a piece of oiled cloth upon the floor. There the vagrant was left to pass the night.

By the light of the candle he examined the room. A bed, with the covers neatly turned back, revealed snowy pillows and sheets. A worn, but clean, red carpet covered the floor. There was a dresser with a beveled mirror, a washstand with a flowered bowl and pitcher; the two or three chairs were softly upholstered. A little table held books, papers, and a day-old cluster of roses in a jar. There were towels on a rack and soap in a white dish.

Whistling Dick set his candle on a chair and placed his hat carefully under the table. After satisfying what we must suppose to have been his curiosity by a sober scrutiny, he removed his coat, folded it, and laid it upon the floor, near the wall, as far as possible from the unused bathtub. Taking his coat for a pillow, he stretched himself luxuriously upon the carpet.

When, on Christmas morning, the first streaks of dawn broke above the marshes, Whistling Dick awoke and reached instinctively for his hat. Then he remembered that the skirts of Fortune had swept him into their folds on the night previous, and he went to the window and raised it, to let the fresh breath of the morning cool his brow and fix the yet dreamlike memory of his good luck within his brain.

As he stood there, certain dread and ominous sounds pierced the fearful hollow of his ear.

The force of plantation workers, eager to complete the shortened task allotted to them, were all astir. The mighty din of the ogre Labor shook the earth, and the poor tattered and forever disguised Prince in search of his fortune held tight to the window-sill even in the enchanted castle, and trembled.

Already from the bosom of the mill came the thunder of rolling barrels of sugar, and (prison-like sounds) there was a great rattling of chains as the mules were harried with stimulant imprecations to their places by the wagon-tongues. A little vicious "dummy" engine, with a train of flat cars in tow, stewed and fumed on the plantation tap of the narrow-gauge railroad, and a toiling, hurrying, hallooing stream of workers were dimly seen in the half darkness loading the train with the weekly output of sugar. Here was a poem, an epic--nay, a tragedy--with work, the curse of the world, for its theme.

The December air was frosty, but the sweat broke out upon Whistling Dick's face. He thrust his head out of the window and looked down. Fifteen feet below him, against the wall of the house, he could make out that a border of flowers grew, and by that token he overhung a bed of soft earth.

Softly as a burglar goes, he clambered out upon the sill, lowered himself until he hung by his hands alone, and then dropped safely. No one seemed to be about upon this side of the house. He dodged low and skimmed swiftly across the yard to the low fence. It was an easy matter to vault this, for a terror urged him such as lifts the gazelle over the thorn bush when the lion pursues. A crash through the dew-drenched weeds on the roadside, a clutching, slippery rush up the grassy side of the levee to the footpath at the summit, and--he was free!

The east was blushing and brightening. The wind, himself a vagrant rover, saluted his brother upon the cheek. Some wild geese, high above, gave cry. A rabbit skipped along the path before him, free to turn to the right or to the left as his mood should send him. The river slid past, and certainly no one could tell the ultimate abiding place of its waters.

A small, ruffled, brown-breasted bird, sitting upon a dogwood sapling, began a soft, throaty, tender little piping in praise of the dew which entices foolish worms from their holes; but suddenly he stopped, and sat with his head turned sidewise, listening.

From the path along the levee there burst forth a jubilant, stirring, buoyant, thrilling whistle, loud and keen and clear as the cleanest notes of the piccolo. The soaring sound rippled and trilled and arpeggioed as the songs of wild birds do not; but it had a wild free grace that, in a way, reminded the small brown bird of something familiar, but exactly what he could not tell. There was in it the bird call, or reveille, that all birds know; but a great waste of lavish, unmeaning things that art had added and arranged, besides, and that were quite puzzling and strange; and the little brown bird sat with his head on one side until the sound died away in the distance.

The little bird did not know that the part of that strange warbling that he understood was just what kept the warbler without his breakfast; but he knew very well that the part he did not understand did not concern him, so he gave a little flutter of his wings and swooped down like a brown bullet upon a big fat worm that was wriggling along the levee path.

XVII   Christmas Every Day

By William Dean Howells

THE little girl came into her papa's study, as she always did Saturday morning before breakfast, and asked for a story. He tried to beg off that morning, for he was very busy, but she would not let him. So he began:

"Well, once there was a little pig--"

She stopped him at the word. She said she had heard little pig-stories till she was perfectly sick of them.

"Well, what kind of story shall I tell, then?"

"About Christmas. It's getting to be the season."

"Well!" Her papa roused himself. "Then I'll tell you about the little girl that wanted it Christmas every day in the year. How would you like that?"

"First-rate!" said the little girl; and she nestled into comfortable shape in his lap, ready for listening.

"Very well, then, this little pig--Oh, what are you pounding me for?"

"Because you said little pig instead of little girl."

"I should like to know what's the difference between a little pig and a little girl that wanted it Christmas every day!"

"Papa!" said the little girl warningly. At this her papa began to tell the story.

Once there was a little girl who liked Christmas so much that she wanted it to be Christmas every day in the year, and as soon as Thanksgiving was over she began to send postcards to the old Christmas Fairy to ask if she mightn't have it. But the old Fairy never answered, and after a while the little girl found out that the Fairy wouldn't notice anything but real letters sealed outside with a monogram--or your initial, anyway. So, then, she began to send letters, and just the day before Christmas, she got a letter from the Fairy, saying she might have it Christmas every day for a year, and then they would see about having it longer.

The little girl was excited already, preparing for the old-fashioned, once-a-year Christmas that was coming the next day. So she resolved to keep the Fairy's promise to herself and surprise everybody with it as it kept coming true, but then it slipped out of her mind altogether.

She had a splendid Christmas. She went to bed early, so as to let Santa Claus fill the stockings, and in the morning she was up the first of anybody and found hers all lumpy with packages of candy, and oranges and grapes, and rubber balls, and all kinds of small presents. Then she waited until the rest of the family was up, and she burst into the library to look at the large presents laid out on the library table--books, and boxes of stationery, and dolls, and little stoves, and dozens of handkerchiefs, and inkstands, and skates, and photograph frames, and boxes of watercolors, and dolls' houses--and the big Christmas tree, lighted and standing in the middle.

She had a splendid Christmas all day. She ate so much candy that she did not want any breakfast, and the whole forenoon the presents kept pouring in that had not been delivered the night before, and she went round giving the presents she had got for other people, and came home and ate turkey and cranberry for dinner, and plum pudding and nuts and raisins and oranges, and then went out and coasted, and came in with a stomachache crying, and her papa said he would see if his house was turned into that sort of fool's paradise another year, and they had a light supper, and pretty early everybody went to bed cross.

The little girl slept very heavily and very late, but she

was wakened at last by the other children dancing around her bed with their stockings full of presents in their hands. "Christmas! Christmas! Christmas!" they all shouted.

"Nonsense! It was Christmas yesterday," said the little girl, rubbing her eyes sleepily.

Her brothers and sisters just laughed. "We don't know about that. It's Christmas today, anyway. You come into the library and see."

Then all at once it flashed on the little girl that the Fairy was keeping her promise, and her year of Christmases was beginning. She was dreadfully sleepy, but she sprang up and darted into the library. There it was again! Books, and boxes of stationery, and dolls, and so on.

There was the Christmas tree blazing away, and the family picking out their presents, and her father looking perfectly puzzled, and her mother ready to cry. "I'm sure I don't see how I'm to dispose of all these things," said her mother, and her father said it seemed to him they had had something just like it the day before, but he supposed he must have dreamed it. This struck the little girl as the best kind of a joke, and so she ate so much candy she didn't want any breakfast, and went round carrying presents, and had turkey and cranberry for dinner, and then went out and coasted, and came in with a stomachache, crying.

Now, the next day, it was the same thing over again, but everybody getting crosser, and at the end of a week's time so many people had lost their tempers that you could pick up lost tempers anywhere, they perfectly strewed the ground. Even when people tried to recover their tempers they usually got somebody else's, and it made the most dreadful mix.

The little girl began to get frightened, keeping the secret all to herself, she wanted to tell her mother, but she didn't dare to, and she was ashamed to ask the Fairy to take back her gift, it seemed ungrateful and ill-bred. So it went on and on, and it was Christmas on St. Valentine's Day and Washington's Birthday, just the same as any day, and it didn't skip even the First of April, though everything was counterfeit that day, and that was some little relief.

After a while turkeys got to be awfully scarce, selling for about a thousand dollars apiece. They got to passing off almost anything for turkeys--even half-grown hummingbirds. And cranberries--well they asked a diamond apiece for cranberries. All the woods and orchards were cut down for Christmas trees. After a while they had to make Christmas trees out of rags. But there were plenty of rags, because people got so poor, buying presents for one another, that they couldn't get any new clothes, and they just wore their old ones to tatters. They got so poor that everybody had to go to the poorhouse, except the confectioners, and the storekeepers, and the book-sellers, and they all got so rich and proud that they would hardly wait upon a person when he came to buy. It was perfectly shameful!

After it had gone on about three or four months, the little girl, whenever she came into the room in the morning and saw those great ugly, lumpy stockings dangling at the fireplace, and the disgusting presents around everywhere, used to sit down and burst out crying. In six months she was perfectly exhausted, she couldn't even cry anymore.

And how it was on the Fourth of July! On the Fourth of July, the first boy in the United States woke up and found out that his firecrackers and toy pistol and two-dollar collection of fireworks were nothing but sugar and candy painted up to look like fireworks. Before ten o'clock every boy in the United States discovered that his July Fourth things had turned into Christmas things and was so mad. The Fourth of July orations all turned into Christmas carols, and when anybody tried to read the Declaration of Independence, instead of saying, "When in the course of human events it becomes necessary," he was sure to sing, "God rest you merry gentlemen." It was perfectly awful.

About the beginning of October the little girl took to sitting down on dolls wherever she found them--she hated the sight of them so, and by Thanksgiving she just slammed her presents across the room. By that time people didn't carry presents around nicely anymore. They flung them over the fence or through the window, and, instead of taking great pains to write "For dear Papa," or "Mama " or "Brother," or "Sister," they used to write, "Take it, you horrid old thing!" and then go and bang it against the front door.

Nearly everybody had built barns to hold their presents, but pretty soon the barns overflowed, and then they used to let them lie out in the rain, or anywhere. Sometimes the police used to come and tell them to shovel their presents off the sidewalk or they would arrest them.

Before Thanksgiving came it had leaked out who had caused all these Christmases. The little girl had suffered so much that she had talked about it in her sleep, and after that hardly anybody would play with her, because if it had not been for her greediness it wouldn't have happened.

And now, when it came Thanksgiving, and she wanted them to go to church, and have turkey, and show their gratitude, they said that all the turkeys had been eaten for her old Christmas dinners and if she would stop the Christmases, they would see about the gratitude. And the very next day the little girl began sending letters to the Christmas Fairy, and then telegrams, to stop it. But it didn't do any good, and then she got to calling at the Fairy's house, but the girl that came to the door always said, "Not at home," or "Engaged," or something like that, and so it went on till it came to the old once-a-year Christmas Eve. The little girl fell asleep, and when she woke up in the morning--

"She found it was all nothing but a dream," suggested the little girl.

"No indeed!" said her papa. "It was all every bit true!"

"What did she find out, then?'"

"Why, that it wasn't Christmas at last, and wasn't ever going to be, anymore. Now it's time for breakfast."

The little girl held her papa fast around the neck.

"You shan't go if you're going to leave it so!"

"How do you want it left?"

"Christmas once a year."

"All right," said her papa, and he went on again.

Well, with no Christmas ever again, there was the greatest rejoicing all over the country. People met together everywhere and kissed and cried for joy. Carts went around and gathered up all the candy and raisins and nuts, and dumped them into the river, and it made the fish perfectly sick. And the whole United States, as far out as Alaska, was one blaze of bonfires, where the children were burning up their presents of all kinds. They had the greatest time!

The little girl went to thank the old Fairy because she had stopped its being Christmas, and she said she hoped the Fairy would keep her promise and see that Christmas never, never came again. Then the Fairy frowned, and said that now the little girl was behaving just as greedily as ever, and she'd better look out. This made the little girl think it all over carefully again, and she said she would be willing to have it Christmas about once in a thousand years, and then she said a hundred, and then she said ten, and at last she got down to one.

Then the Fairy said that was the good old way that had pleased people ever since Christmas began, and she was agreed. Then the little girl said, "What're your shoes made of?" And the Fairy said, "Leather." And the little girl said, "Bargain's done forever," and skipped off, and hippity-hopped the whole way home, she was so glad.

"How will that do?" asked the papa.

"First-rate!" said the little girl, but she hated to have the story stop, and was rather sober. However, her mama put her head in at the door and asked her papa:

"Are you never coming to breakfast? What have you been telling that child?"

"Oh, just a tale with a moral."

The little girl caught him around the neck again.

"We know! Don't you tell what, papa! Don't you tell what!"

XVIII   At Christmas Time

By Anton Chekhov

"WHAT shall I write?" asked Yegor, dipping his pen in the ink.

Vasilissa had not seen her daughter for four years. Efimia had gone away to St. Petersburg with her husband after her wedding, had written two letters, and then had vanished as if the earth had engulfed her, not a word nor a sound had come from her since. So now, whether the aged mother was milking the cow at daybreak, or lighting the stove, or dozing at night, the tenor of her thoughts was always the same: "How is Efimia? Is she alive and well?" She wanted to send her a letter, but the old father could not write, and there was no one whom they could ask to write it for them.

But now Christmas had come, and Vasilissa could endure the silence no longer. She went to the tavern to see Yegor, the innkeeper's wife's brother, who had done nothing but sit idly at home in the tavern since he had come back from military service, but of whom people said that he wrote the most beautiful letters, if only one paid him enough. Vasilissa talked with the cook at the tavern, and with the innkeeper's wife, and finally with Yegor himself, and at last they agreed on a price of fifteen copecks.

So now, on the second day of the Christmas festival, Yegor was sitting at a table in the inn kitchen with a pen in his hand. Vasilissa was standing in front of him, plunged in thought, with a look of care and sorrow on her face. Her husband, Peter, a tall, gaunt old man with a bald, brown head, had accompanied her. He was staring steadily in front of him like a blind man; a pan of pork that was frying on the stove was sizzling and puffing, and seeming to say:

"Hush, hush, hush!" The kitchen was hot and close.

"What shall I write?" Yegor asked again.

"What's that?" asked Vasilissa, looking at him angrily and suspiciously. "Don't hurry me! You are writing this letter for money, not for love! Now then, begin. To our esteemed son-in-law, Andrei Khrisanfltch, and our only and beloved daughter Efimia, we send greetings and love, and the everlasting blessing of their parents."

"All right, fire away!"

"We wish them a happy Christmas. We are alive and well, and we wish the same for you in the name of God, our Father in heaven--our Father in heaven--"

Vasilissa stopped to think, and exchanged glances with the old man.

"We wish the same for you in the name of God, our Father in Heaven--" she repeated and burst into tears.

That was all she could say. Yet she had thought, as she had lain awake thinking night after night, that ten letters could not contain all she wanted to say. Much water had flowed into the sea since their daughter had gone away with her husband, and the old people had been as lonely as orphans, sighing sadly in the night hours, as if they had buried their child. How many things had happened in the village in all these years! How many people had married, how many had died! How long the winters had been, and how long the nights!

"My, but it's hot!" exclaimed Yegor, unbuttoning his waistcoat. "The temperature must be seventy! Well, what next?" he asked.

The old people answered nothing.

"What is your son-in-law's profession?"

"He used to be a soldier, brother; you know that," replied the old man in a feeble voice. "He went into military service at the same time you did. He used to be a soldier, but now he is in a hospital where a doctor treats sick people with water. He is the door-keeper there."

"You can see it written here," said the old woman, taking a letter out of her handkerchief. "We got this from Efimia a long, long time ago. She may not be alive now."

Yegor reflected a moment, and then began to write swiftly.

"Fate has ordained you for the military profession," he wrote, "therefore we recommend you to look into the articles on disciplinary punishment and penal laws of the war department, and to find there the laws of civilisation for members of that department."

When this was written he read it aloud whilst Vasilissa thought of how she would like to write that there had been a famine last year, and that their flour had not even lasted until Christmas, so that they had been obliged to sell their cow; that the old man was often ill, and must soon surrender his soul to God; that they needed money--but how could she put all this into words? What should she say first and what last?

"Turn your attention to the fifth volume of military definitions," Yegor wrote. "The word soldier is a general appellation, a distinguishing term. Both the commander-in-chief of an army and the last infantryman in the ranks are alike called soldiers--"

The old man's lips moved and he said in a low voice:

"I should like to see my little grandchildren!"

"What grandchildren?" asked the old woman crossly. "Perhaps there are no grandchildren."

"No grandchildren? But perhaps there are! Who knows?"

"And from this you may deduce," Yegor hurried on,

"which is an internal, and which is a foreign enemy. Our greatest internal enemy is Bacehus--"

The pen scraped and scratched, and drew long, curly lines like fish-hooks across the paper. Yegor wrote at full speed and underlined each sentence two or three times. He was sitting on a stool with his legs stretched far apart under the table, a fat, lusty creature with a fiery nape and the face of a bulldog. He was the very essence of coarse, arrogant, stiff-necked vulgarity, proud to have been born and bred in a pot-house, and Vasilissa well knew how vulgar he was, but could not find words to express it, and could only glare angrily and suspiciously at him. Her head ached from the sound of his voice and his unintelligible words, and from the oppressive heat of the room, and her mind was confused. She could neither think nor speak, and could only stand and wait for Yegor's pen to stop scratching. But the old man was looking at the writer with unbounded confidence in his eyes. He trusted his old woman who had brought him here, he trusted Yegor, and, when he had spoken of the hydropathic establishment just now, his face had shown that he trusted that, and the heal-ing power of its waters.

When the letter was written, Yegor got up and read it aloud from beginning to end. The old man understood not a word, but he nodded his head confidingly, and said:

"Very good. It runs smoothly. Thank you kindly, it is very good."

They laid three five-copeck pieces on the table and went out. The old man walked away staring straight ahead of him like a blind man, and a look of utmost confidence lay in his eyes, but Vasilissa, as she left the tavern, struck at a dog in her path and exclaimed angrily:

"Ugh--the plague!"

All that night the old woman lay awake full of restless thoughts, and at dawn she rose, said her prayers, and walked eleven miles to the station to post the letter.

II

Doctor Moselweiser's hydropathic establishment was open on New Year's Day as usual; the only difference was that Andrei Khrisaufitch, the doorkeeper, was wearing unusually shiny boots and a uniform trimmed with new gold braid, and that he wished every one who came in a happy New Year.

It was morning. Andrei was standing at the door reading a paper. At ten o'clock precisely an old general came in who was one of the regular visitors of the establishment. Behind him came the postman. Andrei took the general's cloak, and said:

"A happy New Year to your Excellency!"

"Thank you, friend, the same to you!"

And as he mounted the stairs the general nodded toward a closed door and asked, as he did every day, always forgetting the answer:

"And what is there in there?"

"A room for massage, your Excellency."

When the general's footsteps had died away, Andrei looked over the letters and found one addressed to him. He opened it, read a few lines, and then, still looking at his newspaper, sauntered toward the little room down-stairs at the end of a passage where he and his family lived. His wife Efimia was sitting on the bed feeding a baby, her oldest boy was standing at her knee with his curly head in her lap, and a third child was lying asleep on the bed.

Andrei entered their little room, and handed the letter

to his wife, saying:

"This must be from the village."

Then he went out again, without raising his eyes from his newspaper, and stopped in the passage not far from the door. He heard Efimia read the first lines in a trembling voice. She could go no farther, but these were enough. Tears streamed from her eyes and she threw her arms round her eldest child and began talking to him and covering him with kisses. It was hard to tell whether she was laughing or crying.

"This is from granny and granddaddy," she cried-- "from the village--oh, Queen of Heaven!-- Oh! holy saints! The roofs are piled with snow there now--and the trees are white, oh, so white! The little children are out coasting on their dear little sleddies--and granddaddy darling, with his dear bald head is sitting by the big, old, warm stove, and the little brown doggie--oh, my precious chickabiddies--"

Andrei remembered as he listened to her that his wife had given him letters at three or four different times, and had asked him to send them to the village, but important business had always interfered, and the letters had remained lying about unposted.

"And the little white hares are skipping about in the fields now--" sobbed Efimia, embracing her boy with streaming eyes. "Granddaddy dear is so kind and good, and granny is so kind and so full of pity. People's hearts are soft and warm in the village-- There is a little church there, and the men sing in the choir. Oh, take us away from here, Queen of Heaven! Intercede for us, merciful mother!"

Andrei returned to his room to smoke until the next patient should come in, and Efimia suddenly grew still and wiped her eyes; only her lips quivered. She was afraid of him, oh, so afraid! She quaked and shuddered at every look and every footstep of his, and never dared to open her mouth in his presence.

Andrei lit a cigarette, but at that moment a bell rang upstairs. He put out his cigarette, and assuming a very solemn expression, hurried to the front door.

The old general, rosy and fresh from his bath, was descending the stairs.

"And what is there in there?" he asked, pointing to a closed door.

Andrei drew himself up at attention, and answered in a loud voice:

"The hot douche, your Excellency."

Bibliography

Willa Cather's Collected Short Fiction, *edited by Virginia Faulkner, Lincoln: University of Nebraska Press, 1970, ISBN 0-8032-0770-0.*

Thurber: Writings and Drawings, *The Library of America, 1996, ISBN 1-883011-22-1*